AF606831

CALL AND RESPONSE

CHRISTIAN MARCLAY & STEVE BERESFORD

siglio CATSKILL, NEW YORK 2021

On April 11, 2020, I sent Steve Beresford a photograph taken that day while walking through the empty streets of London. The official lockdown in response to the coronavirus pandemic had started on March 23, and by then the city was a ghost town. The silence was at first spooky, but eventually it felt peaceful. I took this picture because the decorative white balls, irregularly placed on the black fence, reminded me of a musical score. Instantly I thought of Steve confined alone in his flat. I texted him the image with the caption "How would this sound on the piano?" He responded, "Leave it with me. I'll send you something this evening." A few hours later I received a beautiful interpretation that Steve recorded on his phone. This is how our little game started. After a few of these spontaneous exchanges, I realized that all my pictures were of enclosures: gates, fences, windows, closed and boarded-up storefronts. A view of the world behind barriers. Steve responded imaginatively and mournfully to these images of confinement. Later he carefully transcribed the recordings for this book. The twenty short musical compositions are presented here next to the photographs that inspired them.

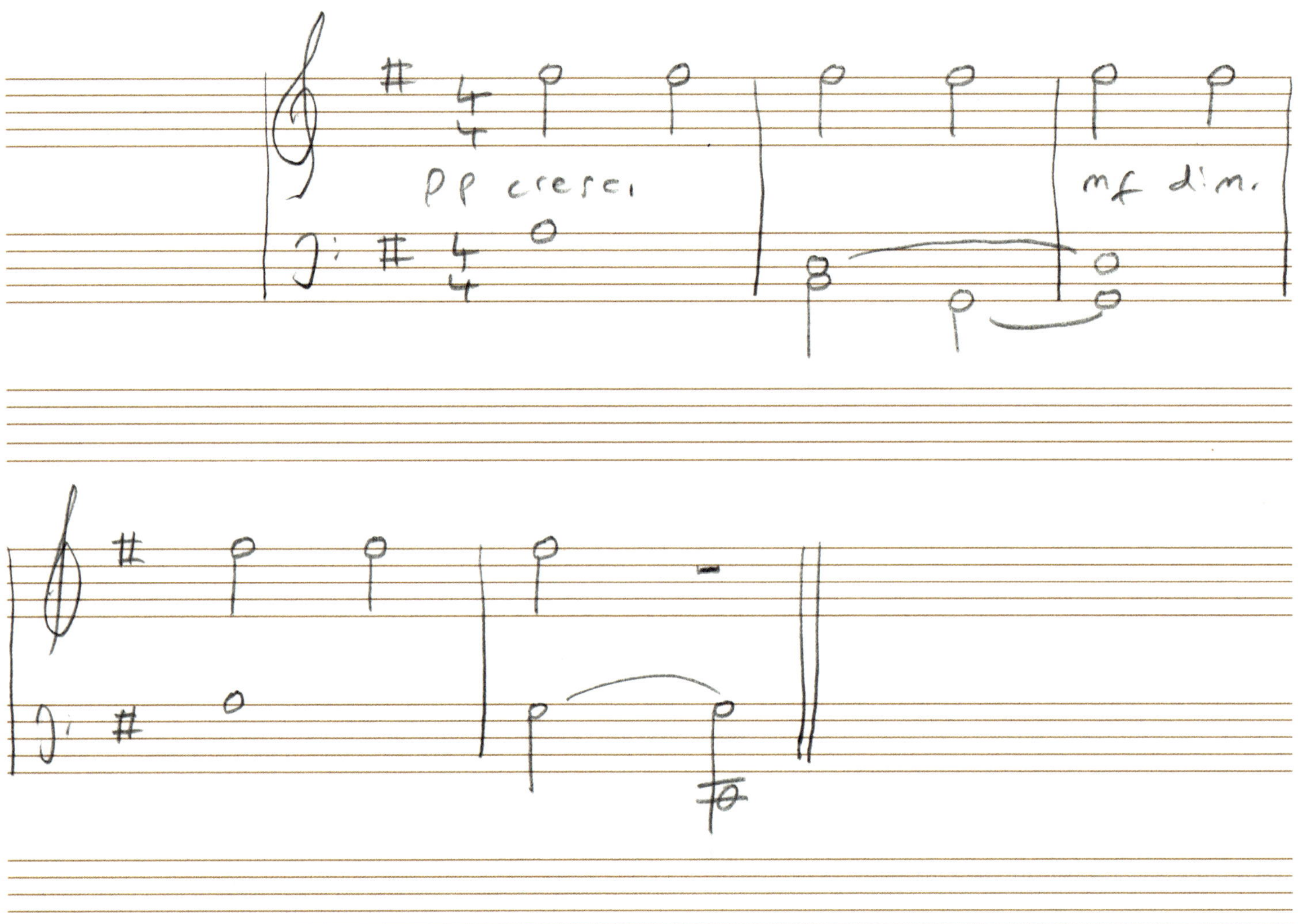
pp cresc.
mf dim.

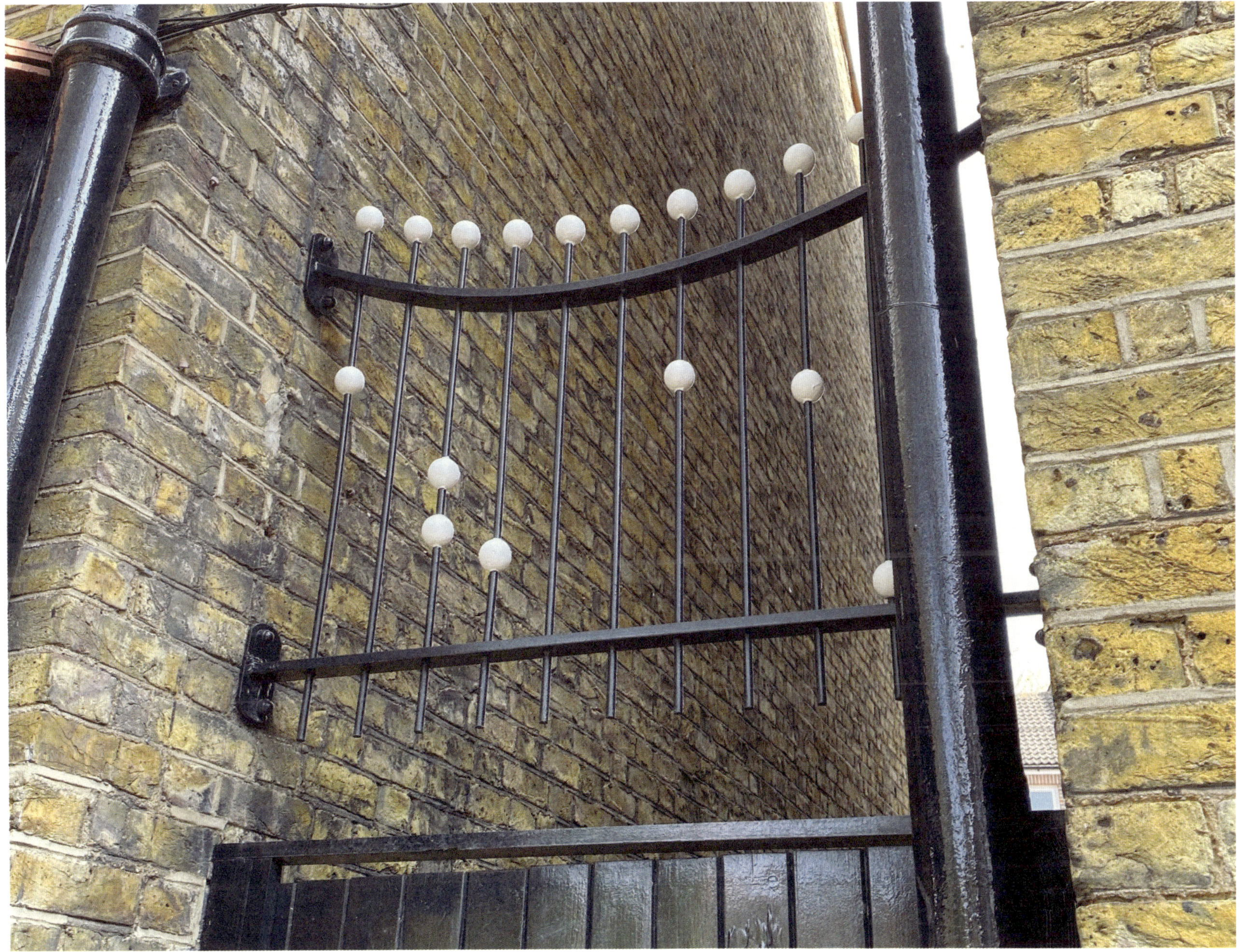

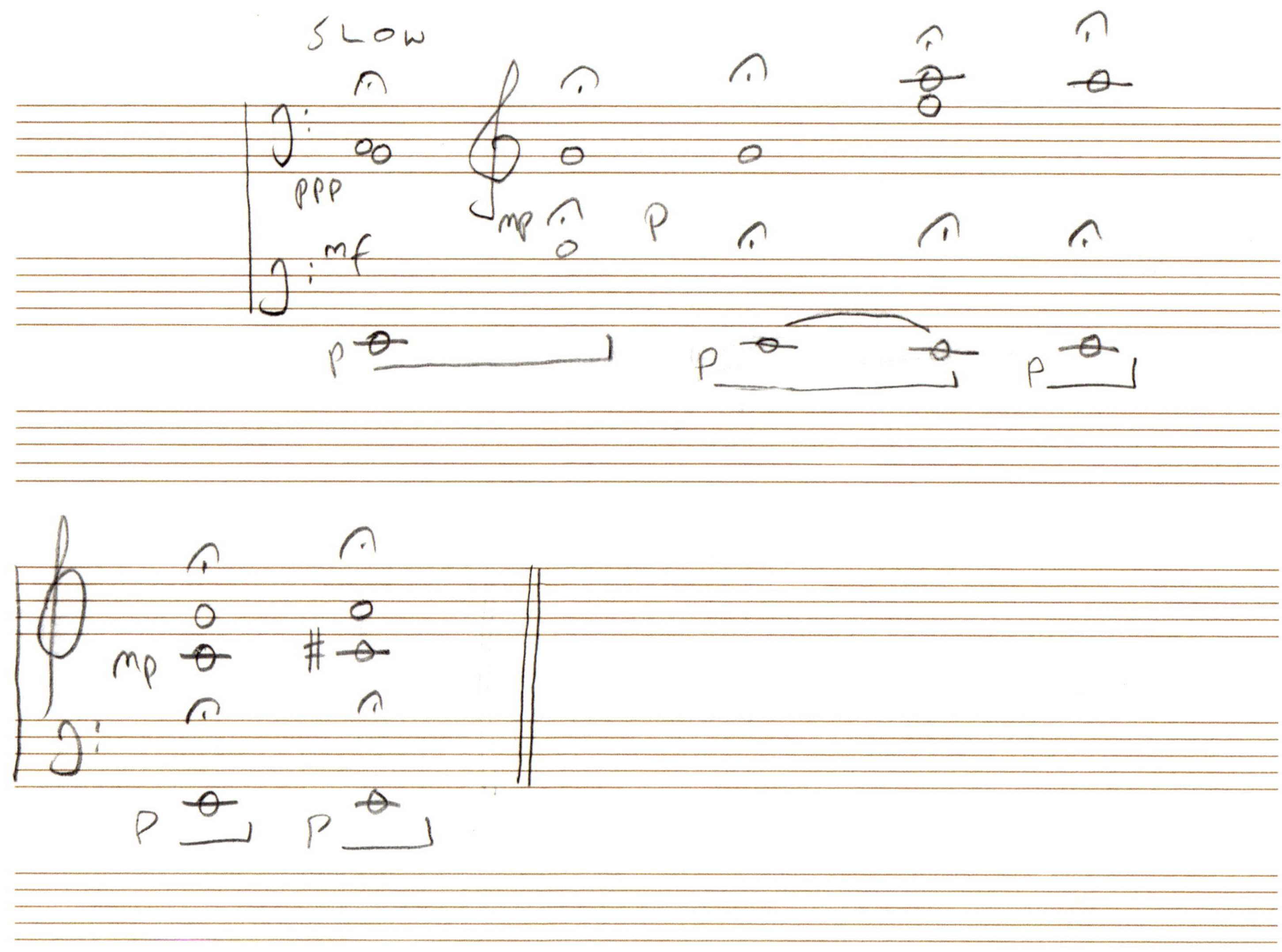

SLOW
ppp
mf
mp
p
p
p
p
mp
p
p

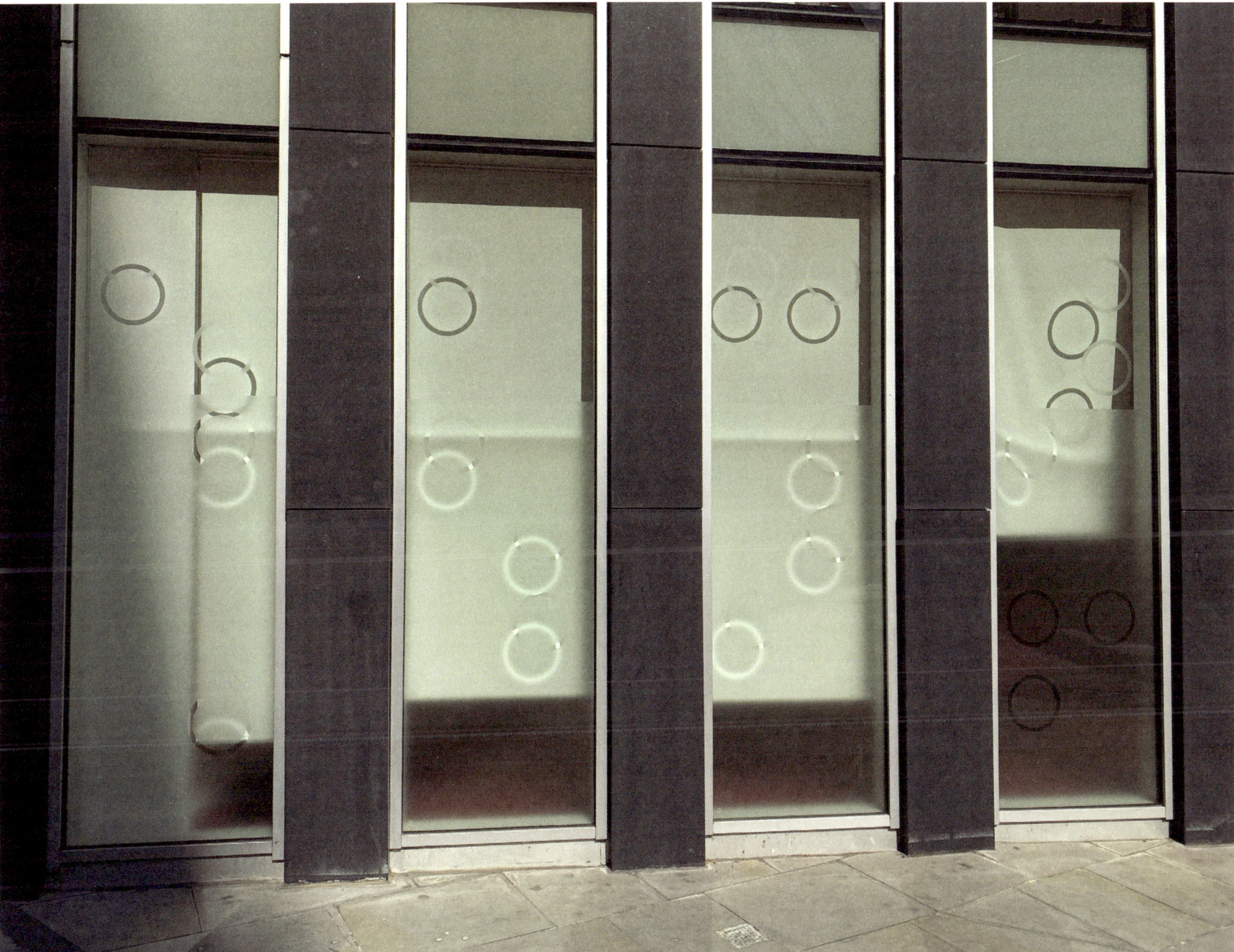

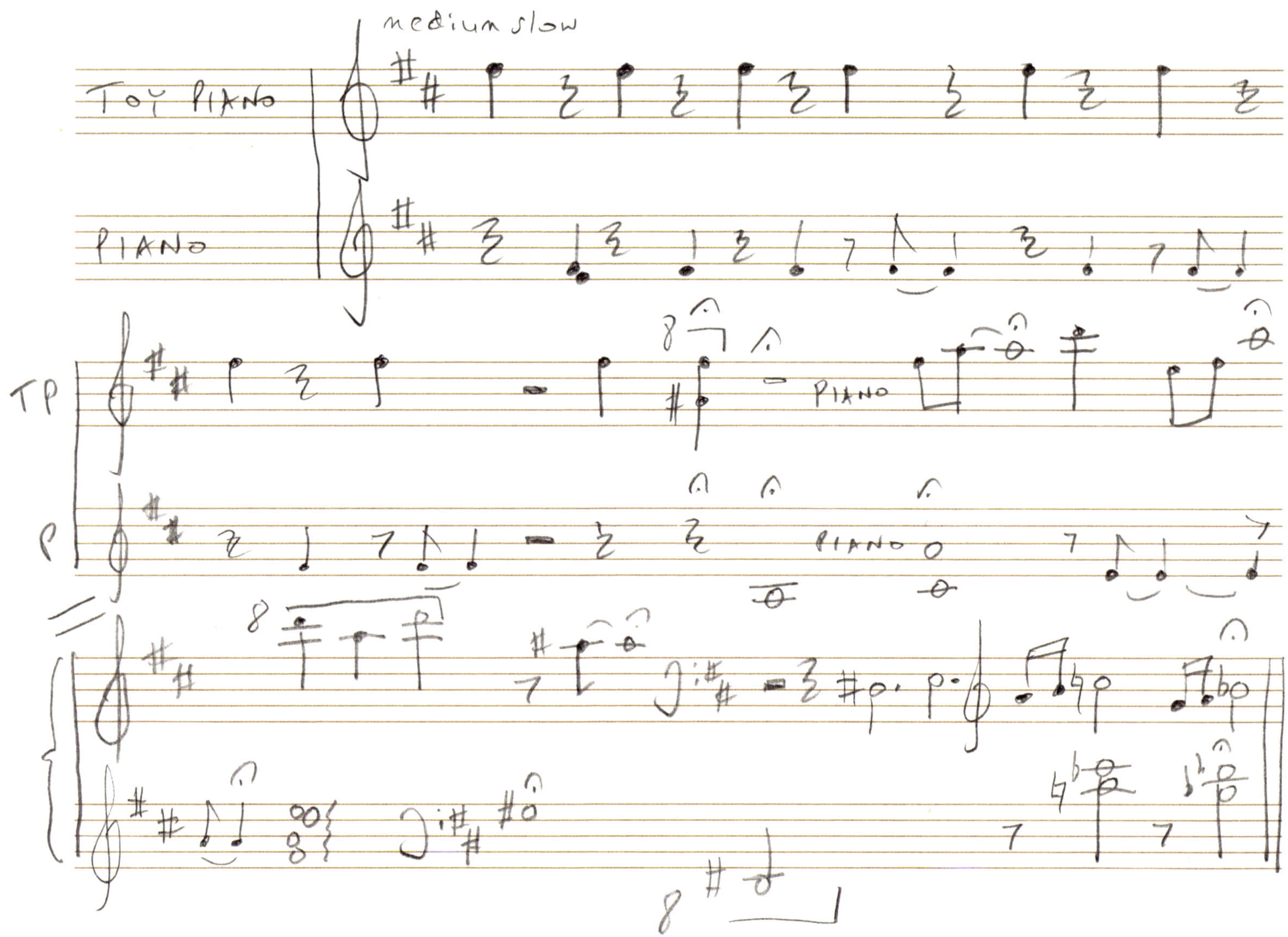
medium slow
TOY PIANO
PIANO
TP
P
PIANO
PIANO
8
8
8

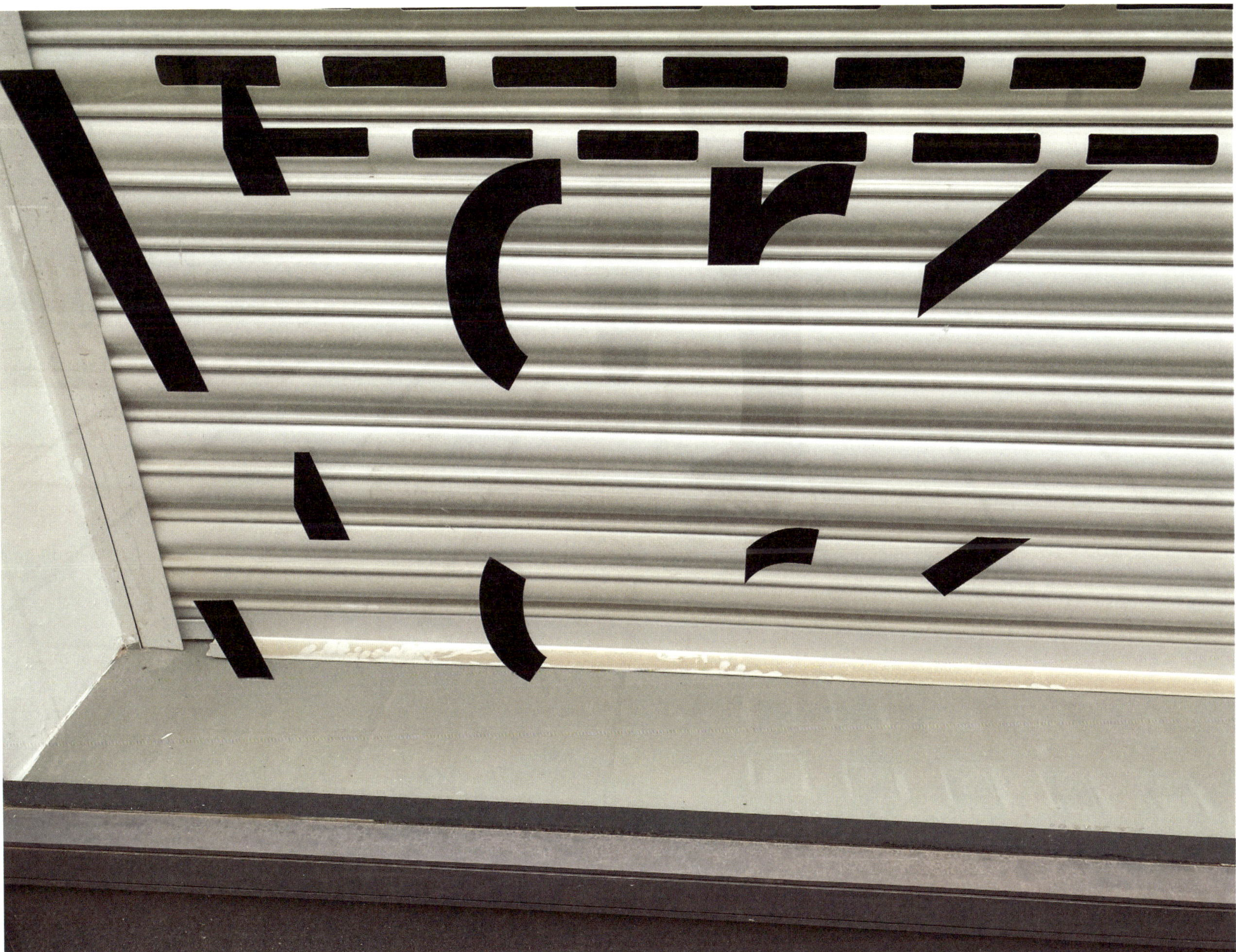

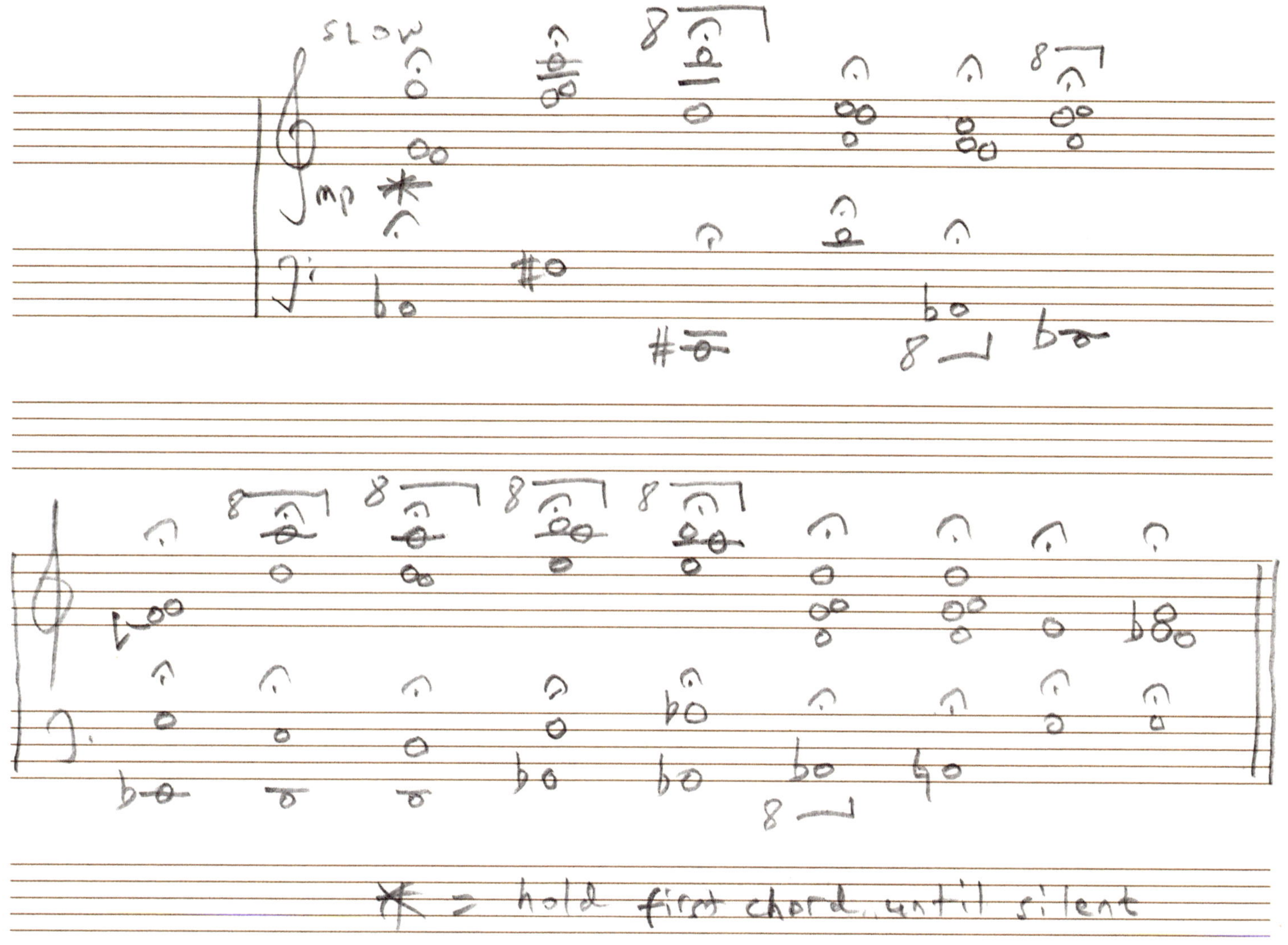
SLOW
mp
8
* = hold first chord until silent

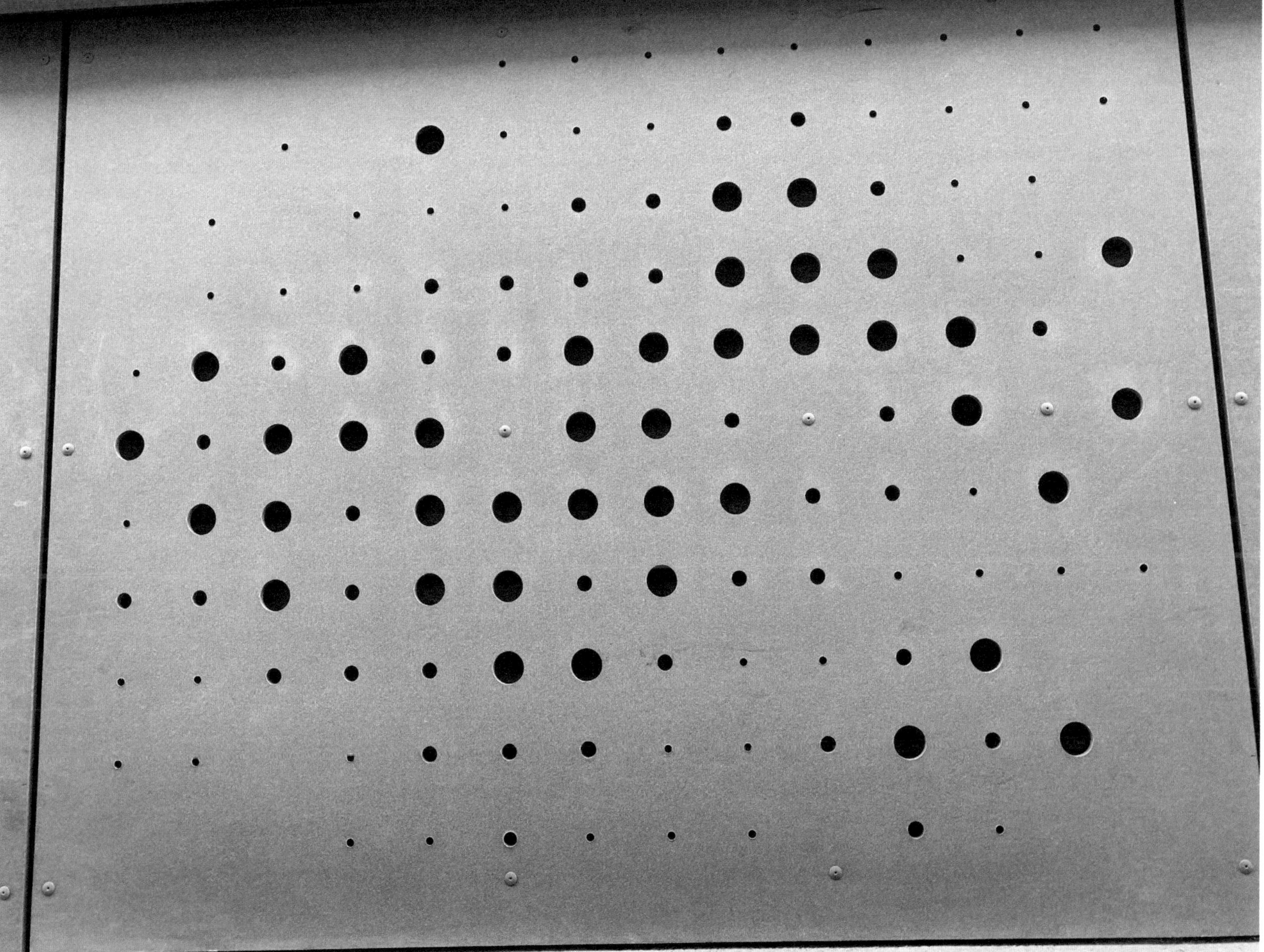

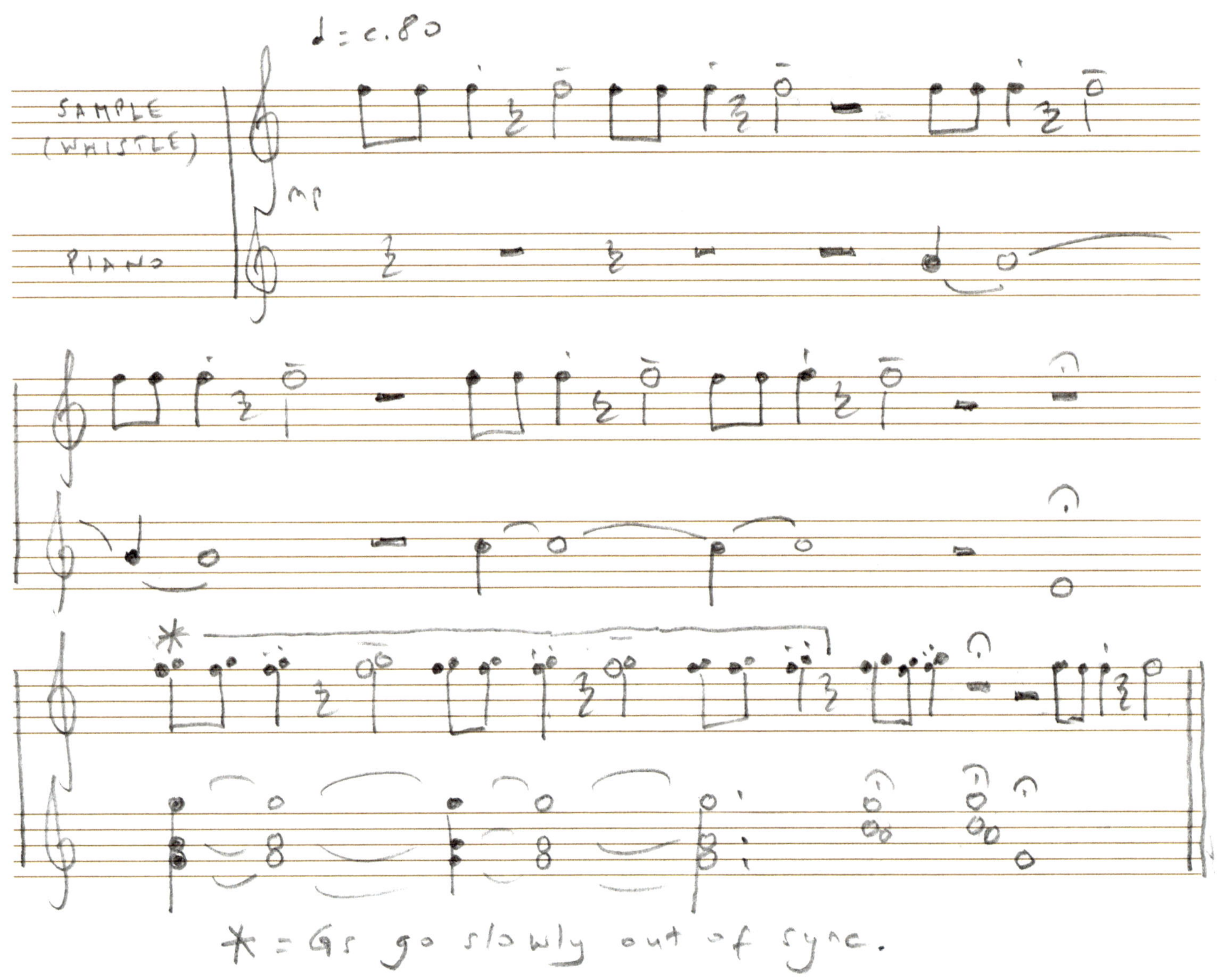
♩ = c.80
SAMPLE (WHISTLE)
PIANO
mp
* = Gs go slowly out of sync.

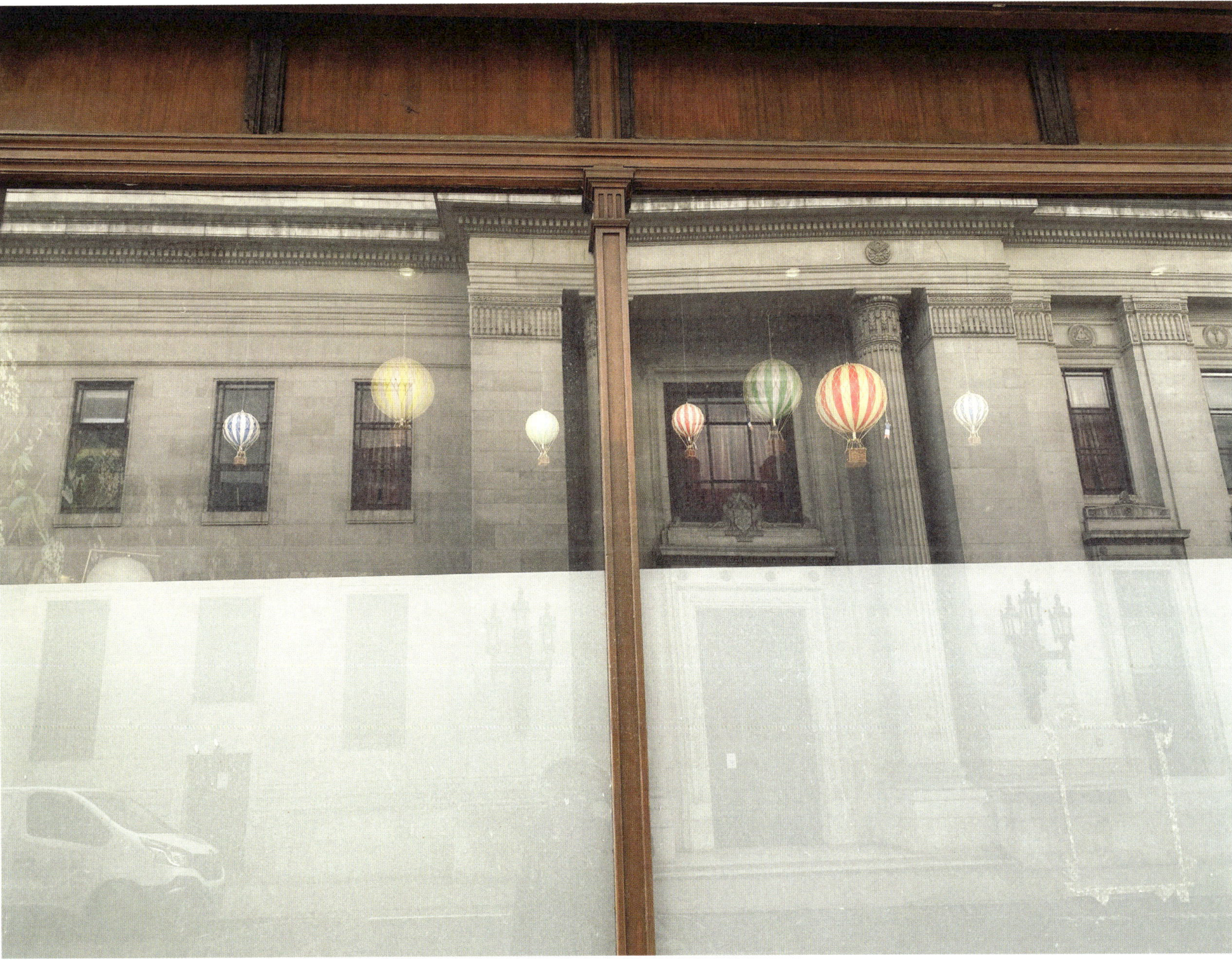

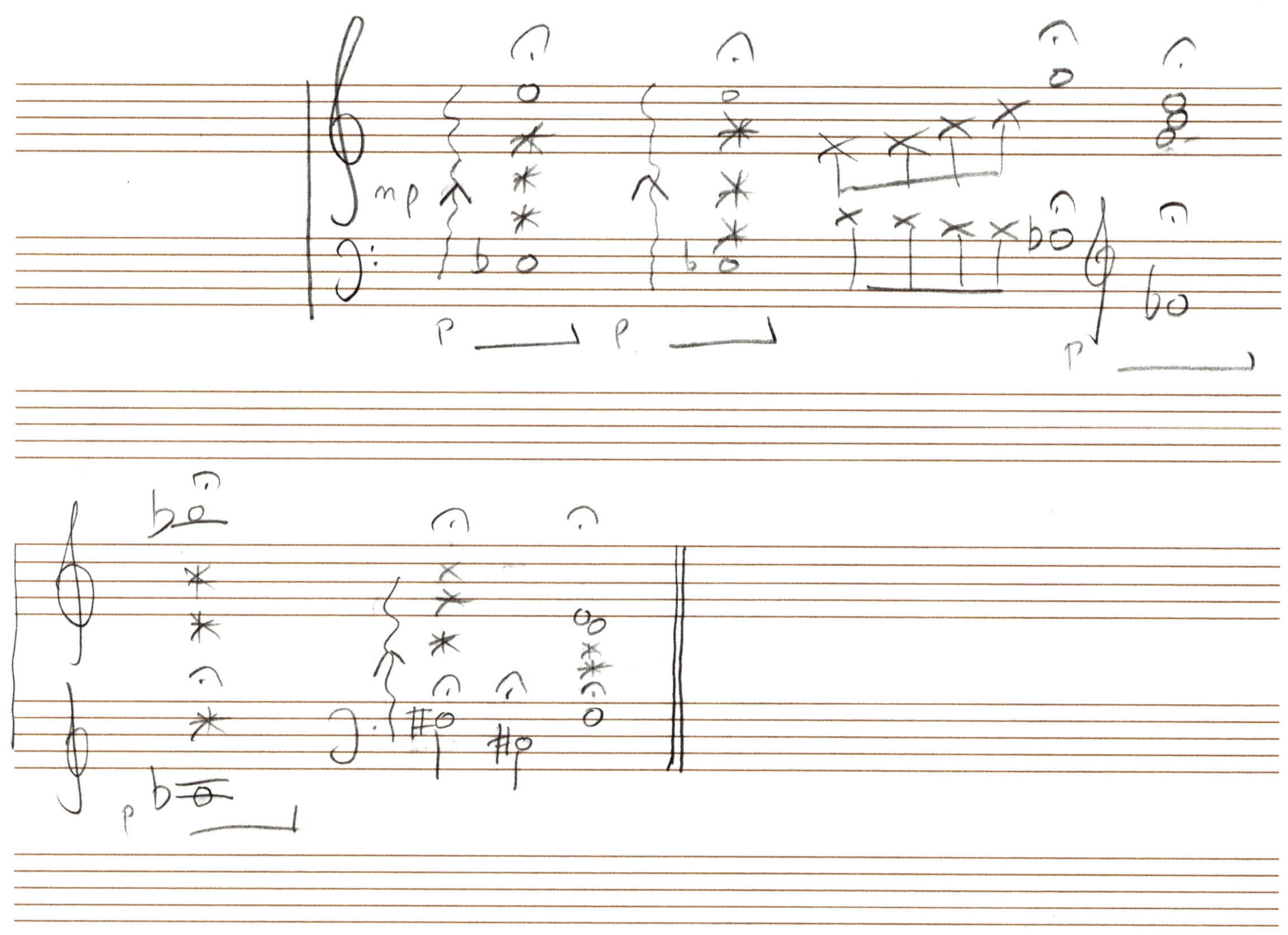

✱ = any nearby notes   X = any nearby note

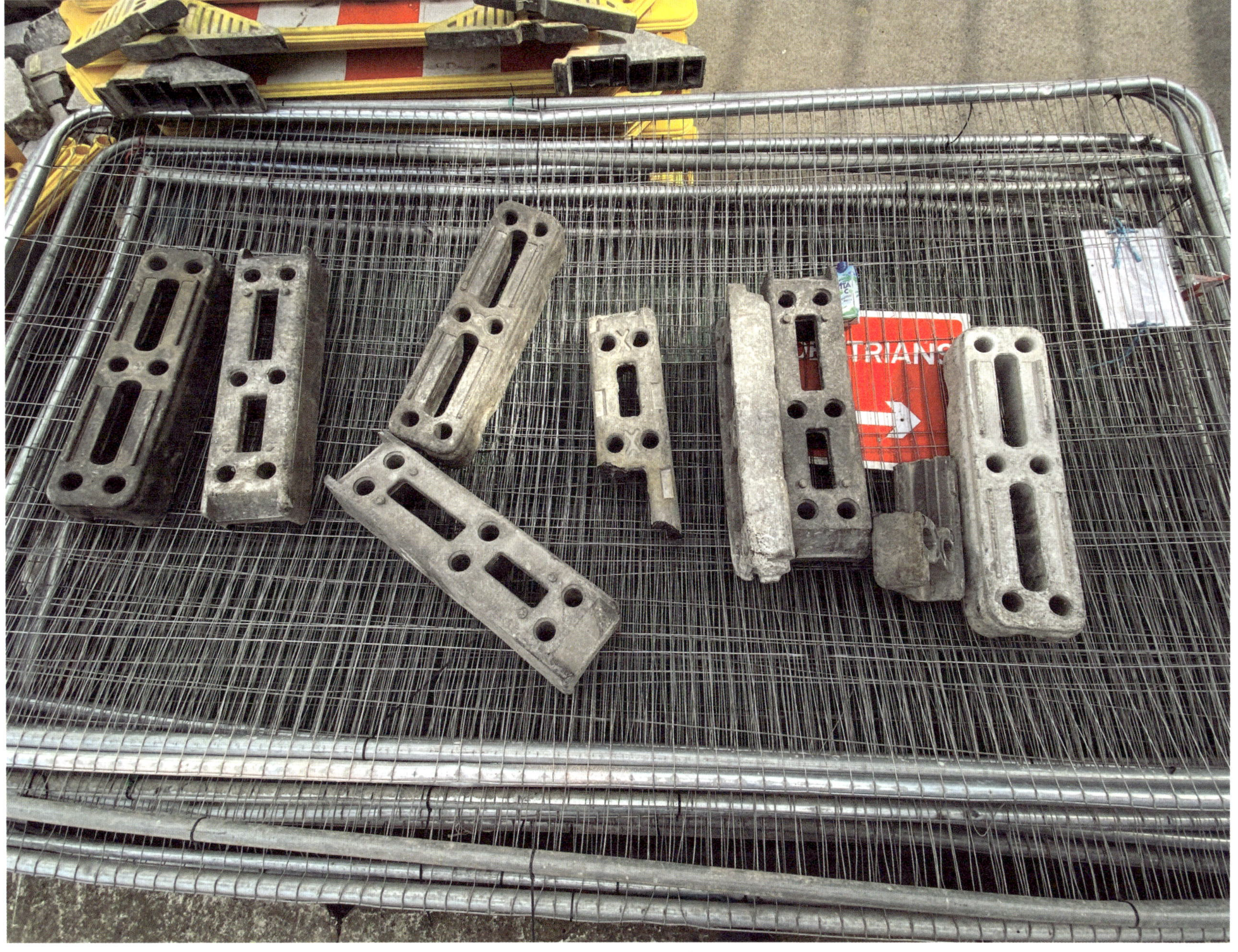

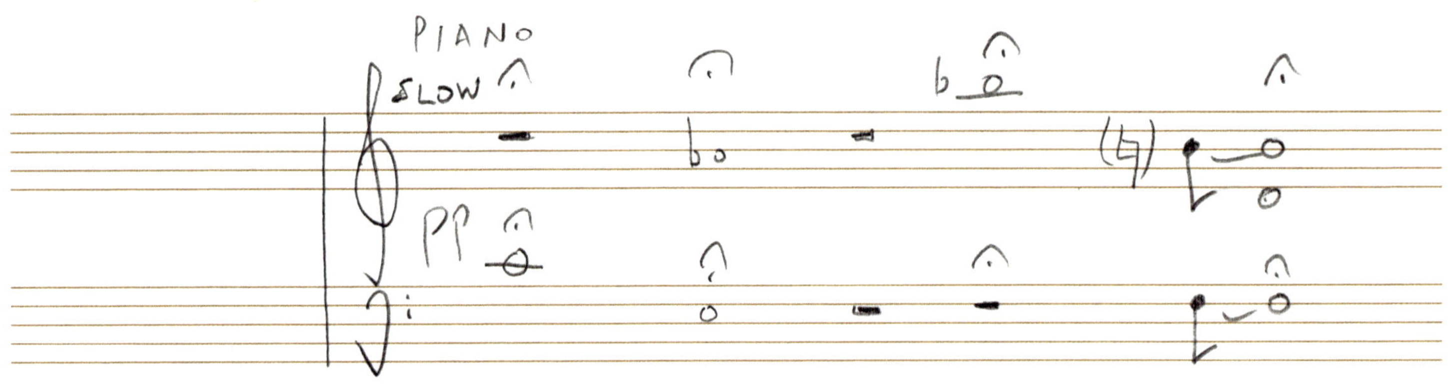
PIANO
SLOW
PP

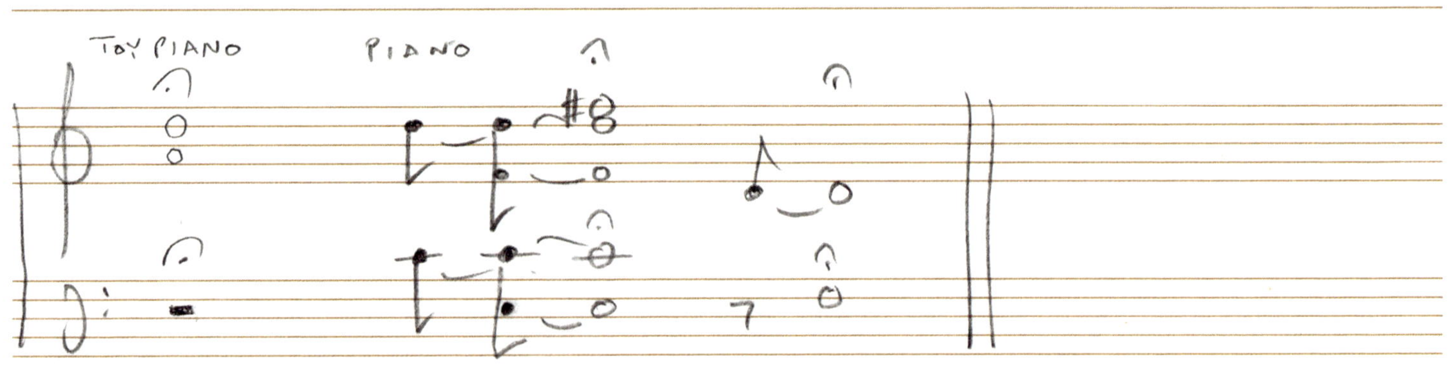
TOY PIANO
PIANO

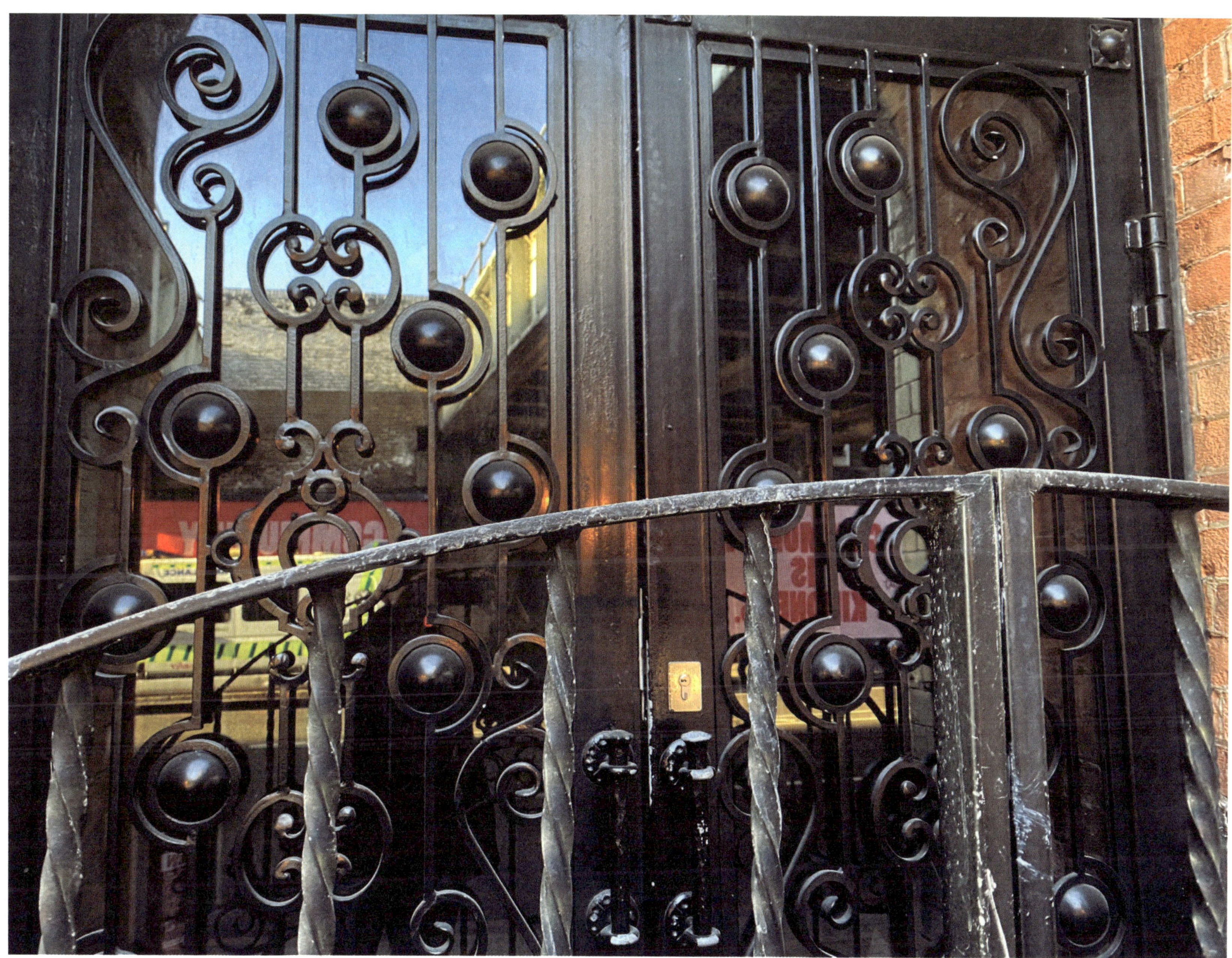

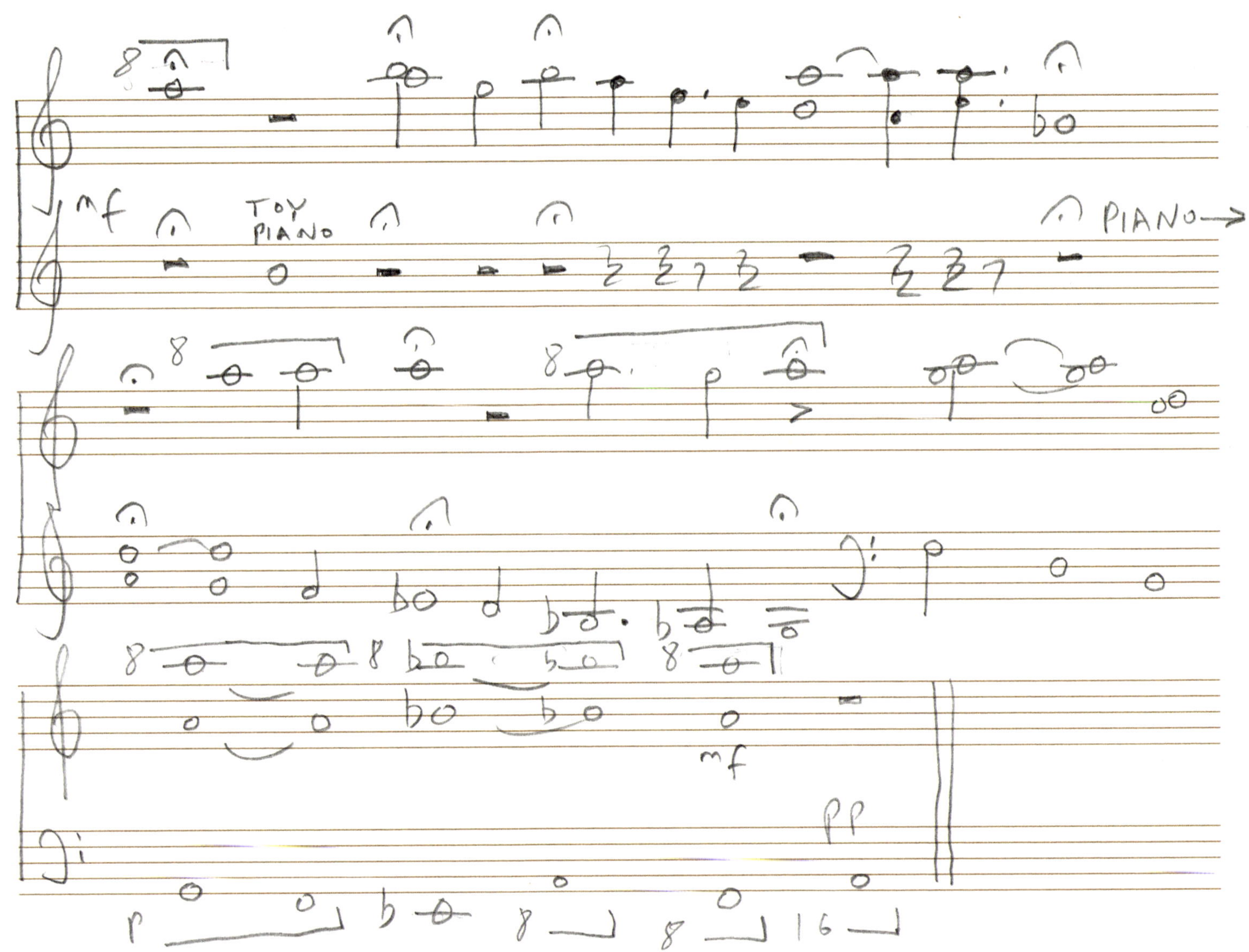
mf
TOY PIANO
PIANO
mf
pp

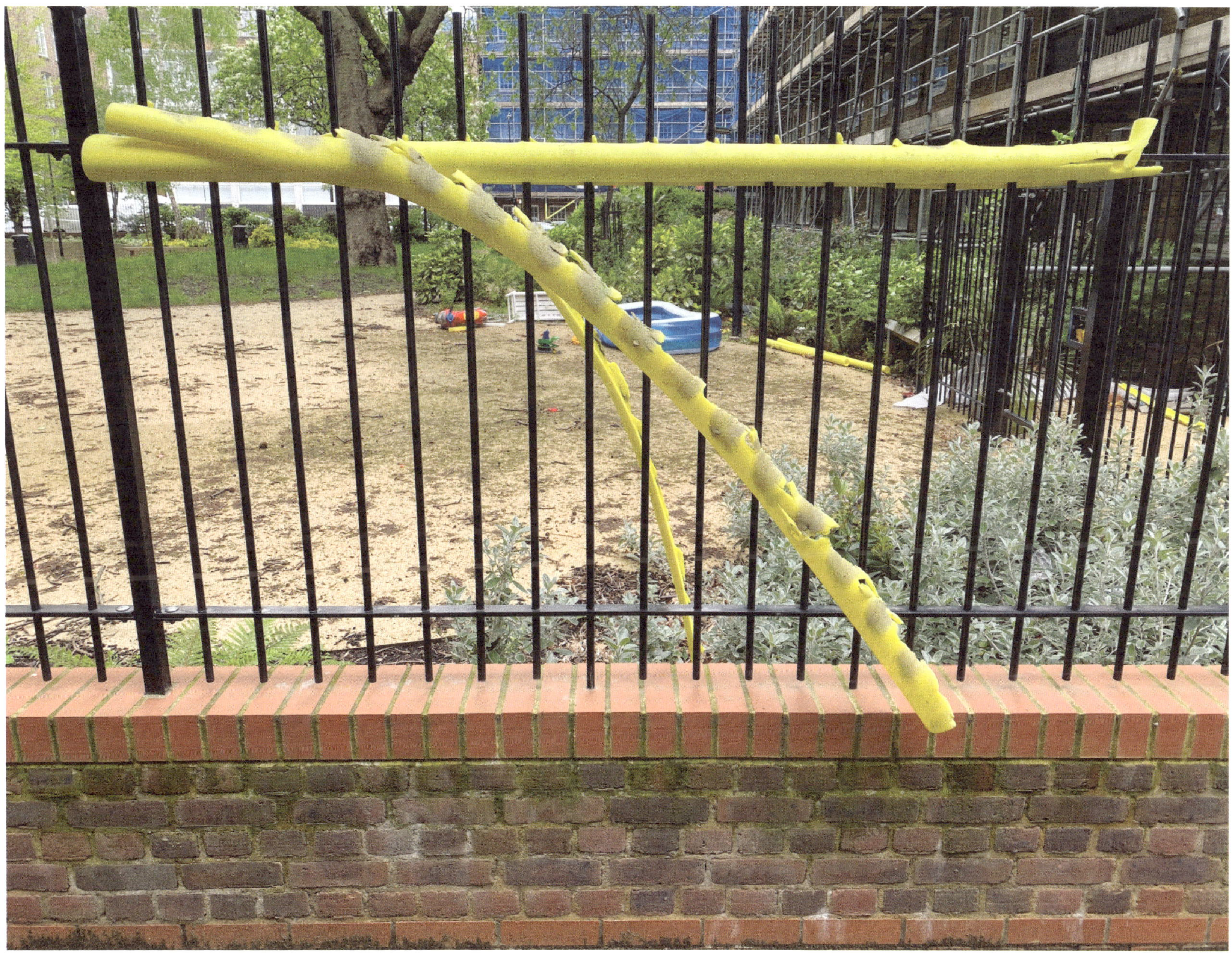

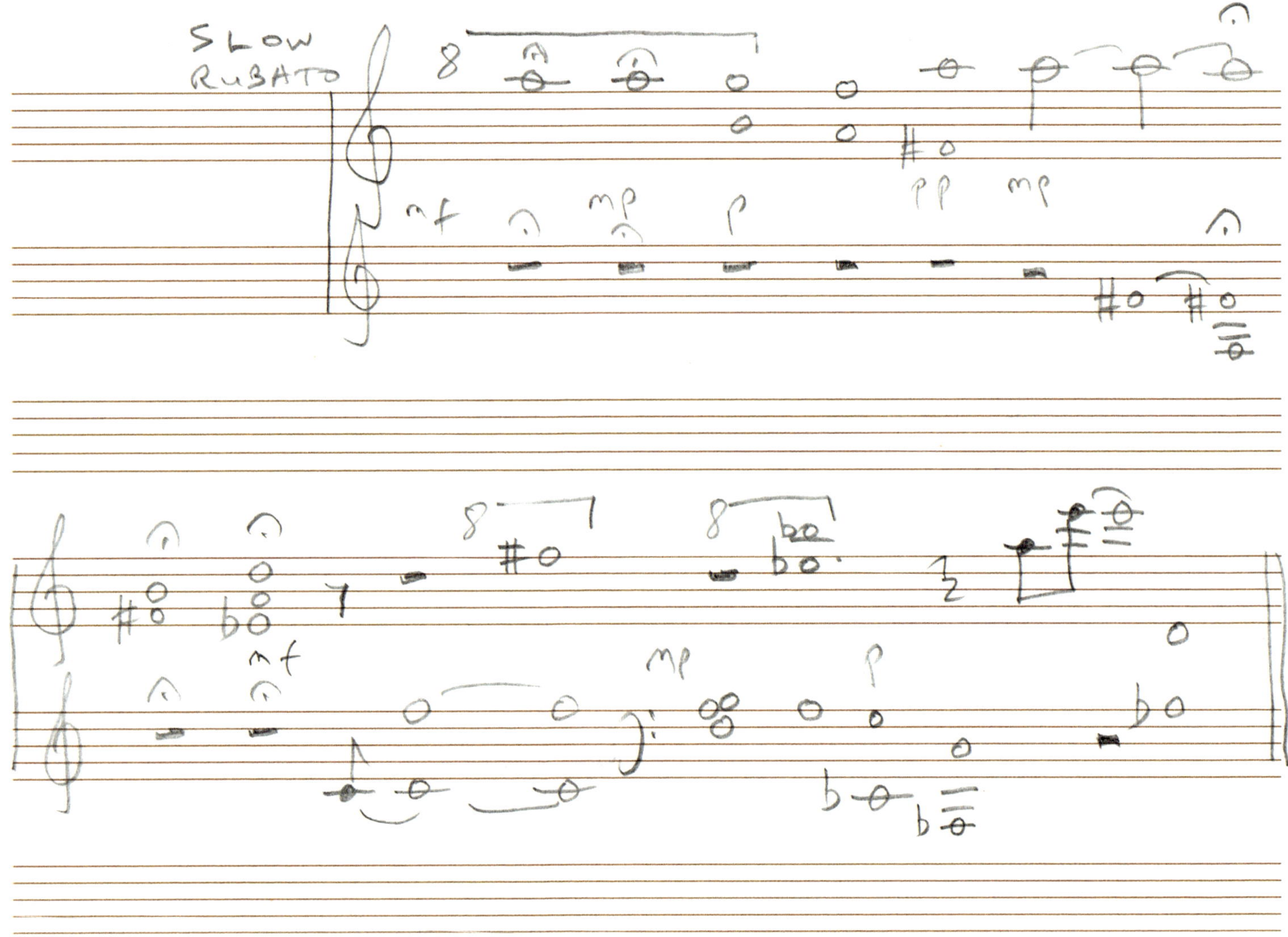
SLOW
RUBATO
8
mf
mp
p
pp
mp
mf
8
8
mp
p

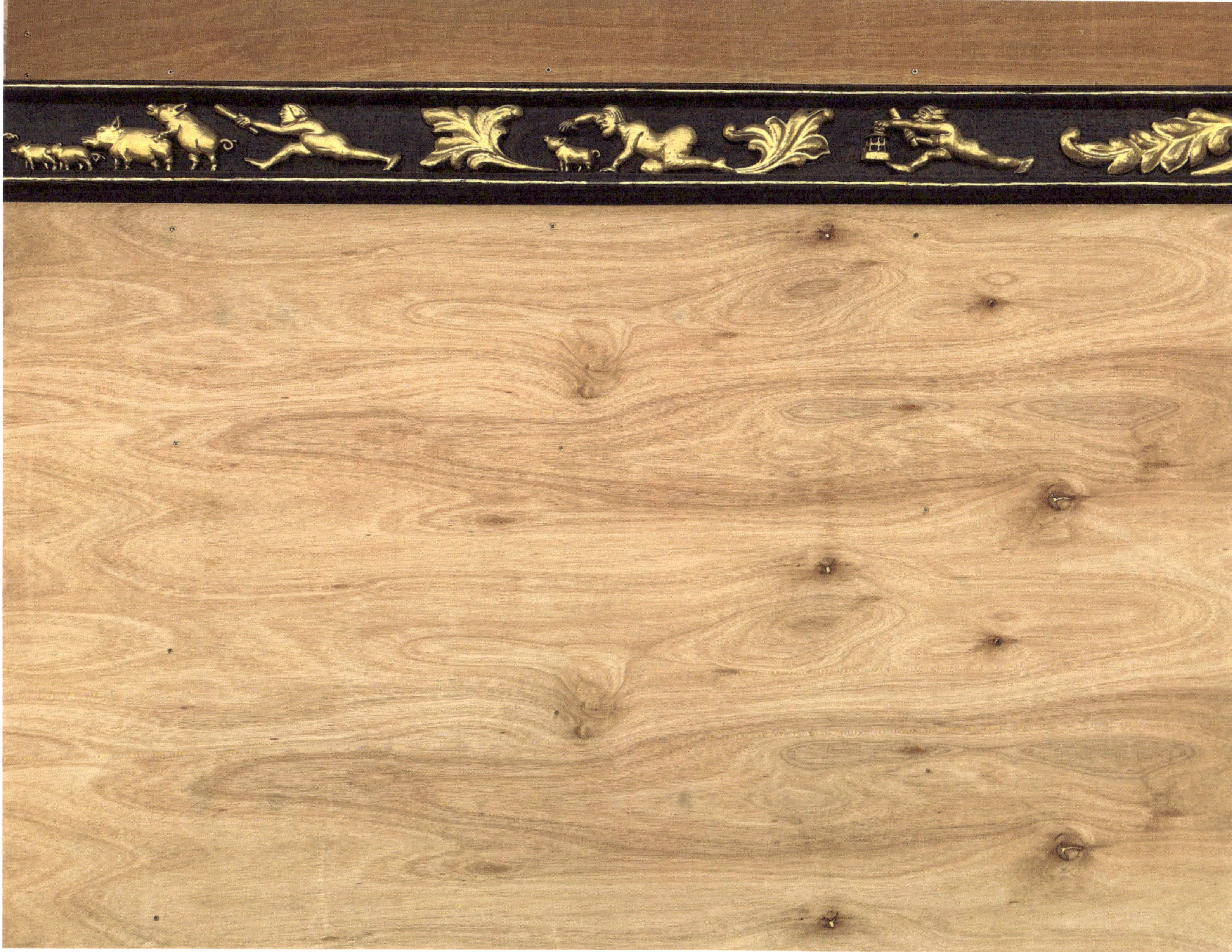

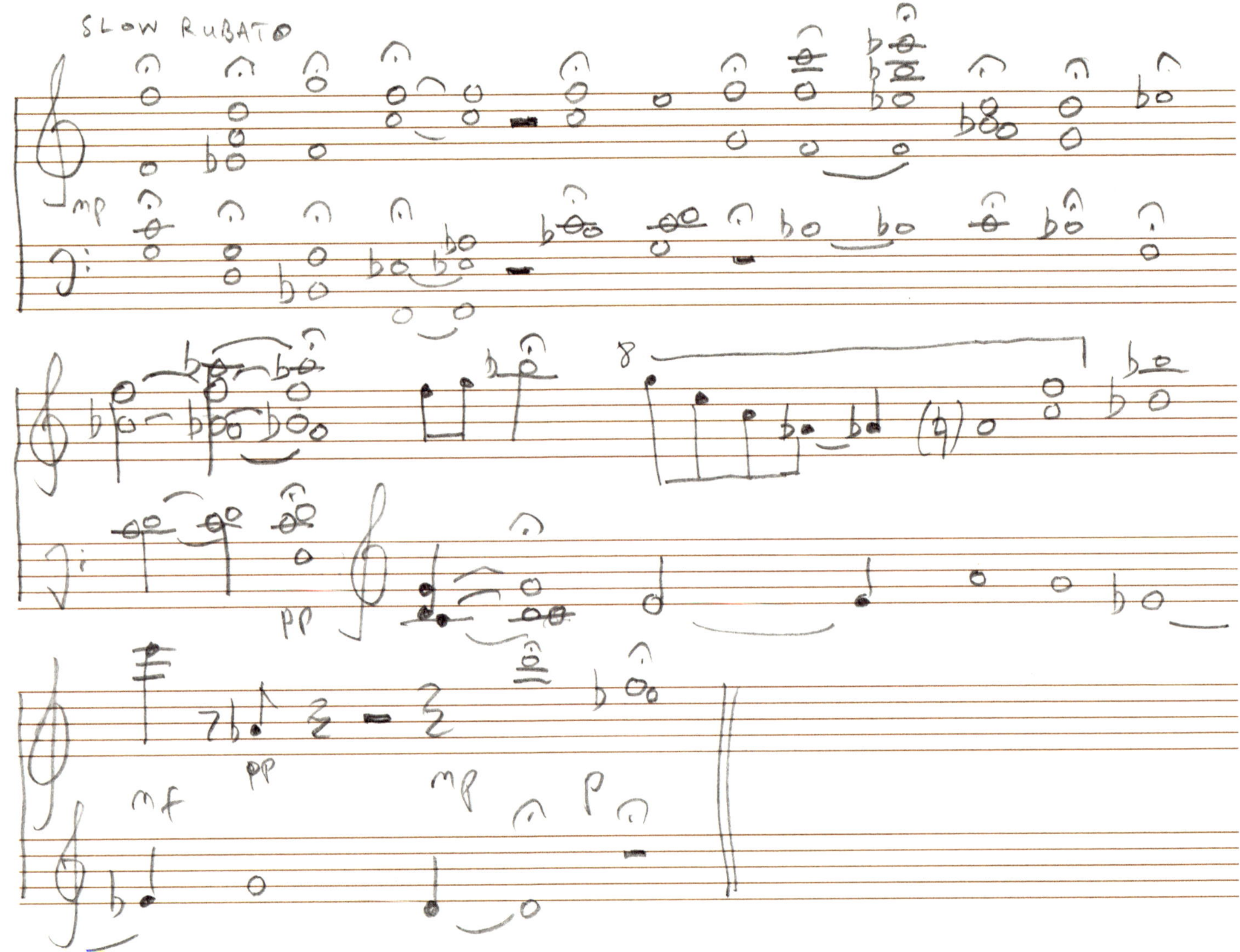
SLOW RUBATO
mp
8
pp
mf
pp
mp
p

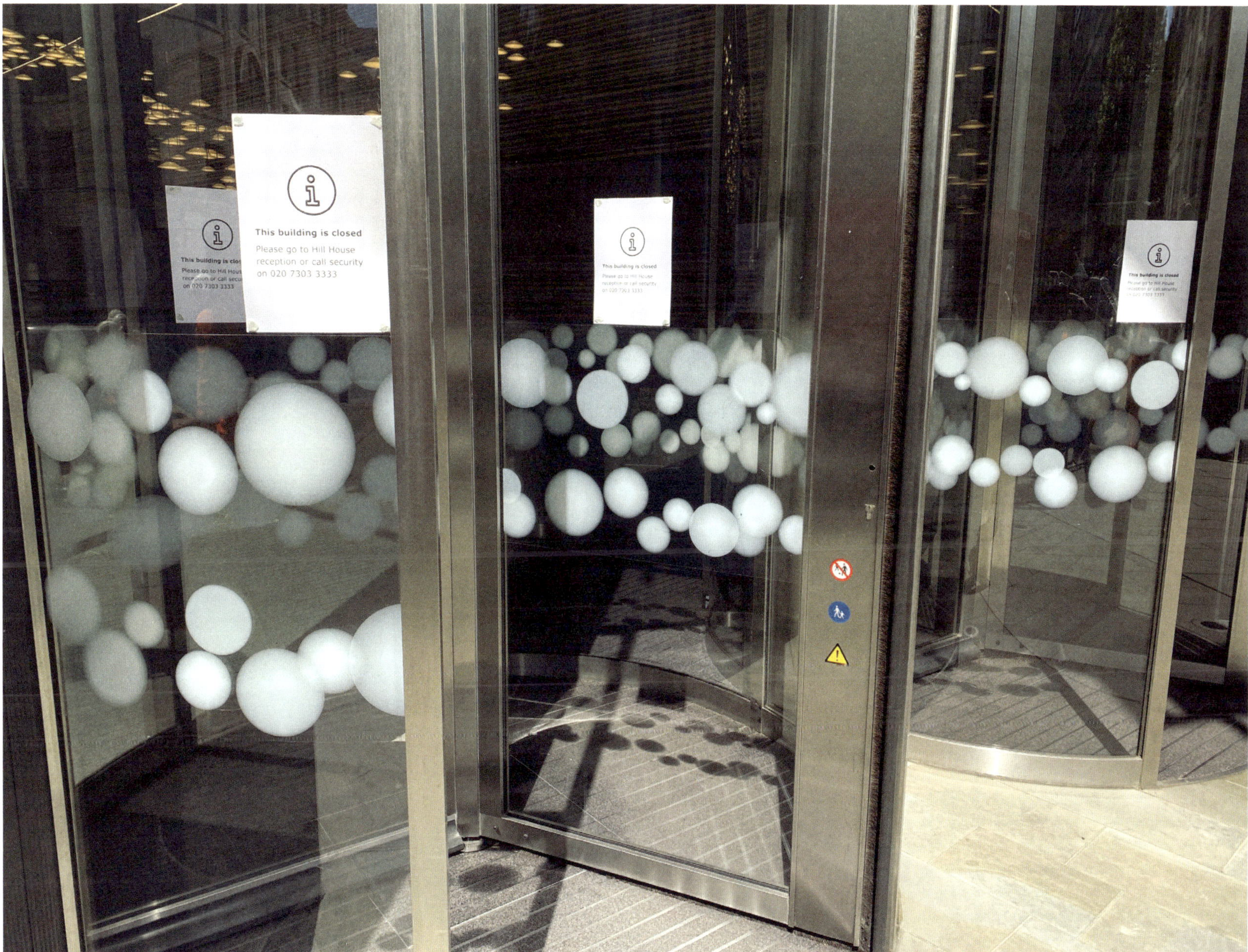
This building is closed
Please go to Hill House
reception or call security
on 020 7303 3333

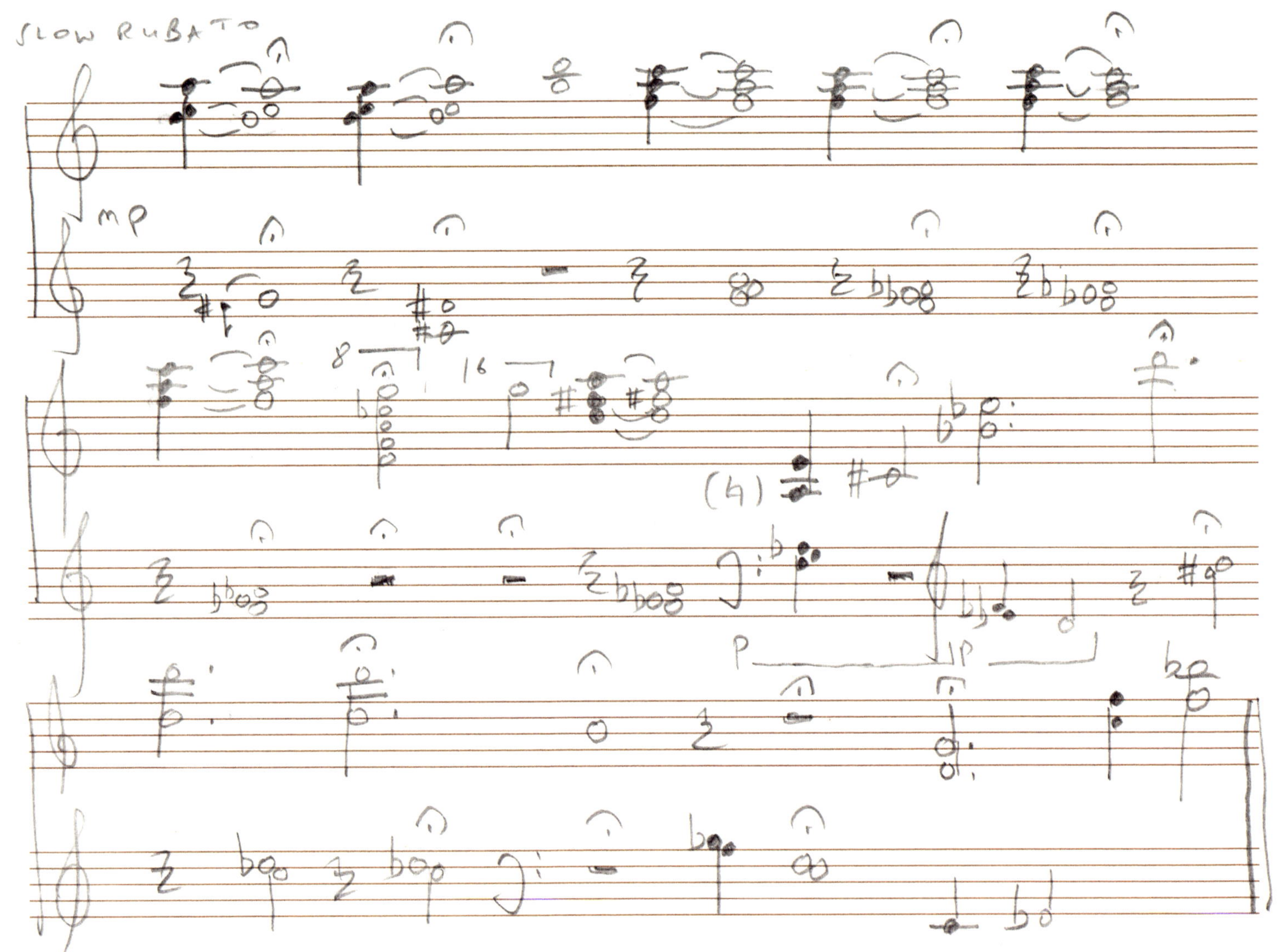

11

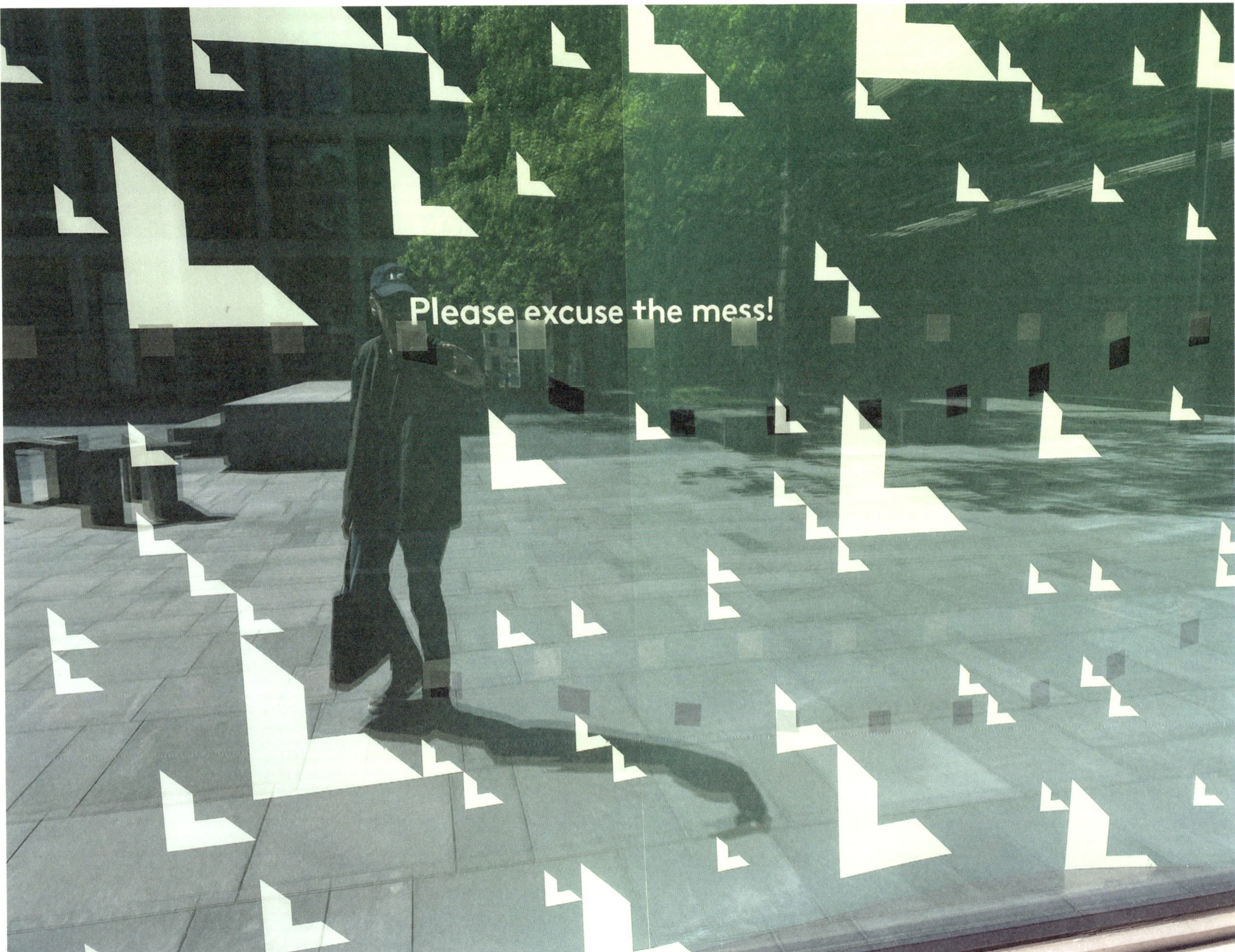
Please excuse the mess!

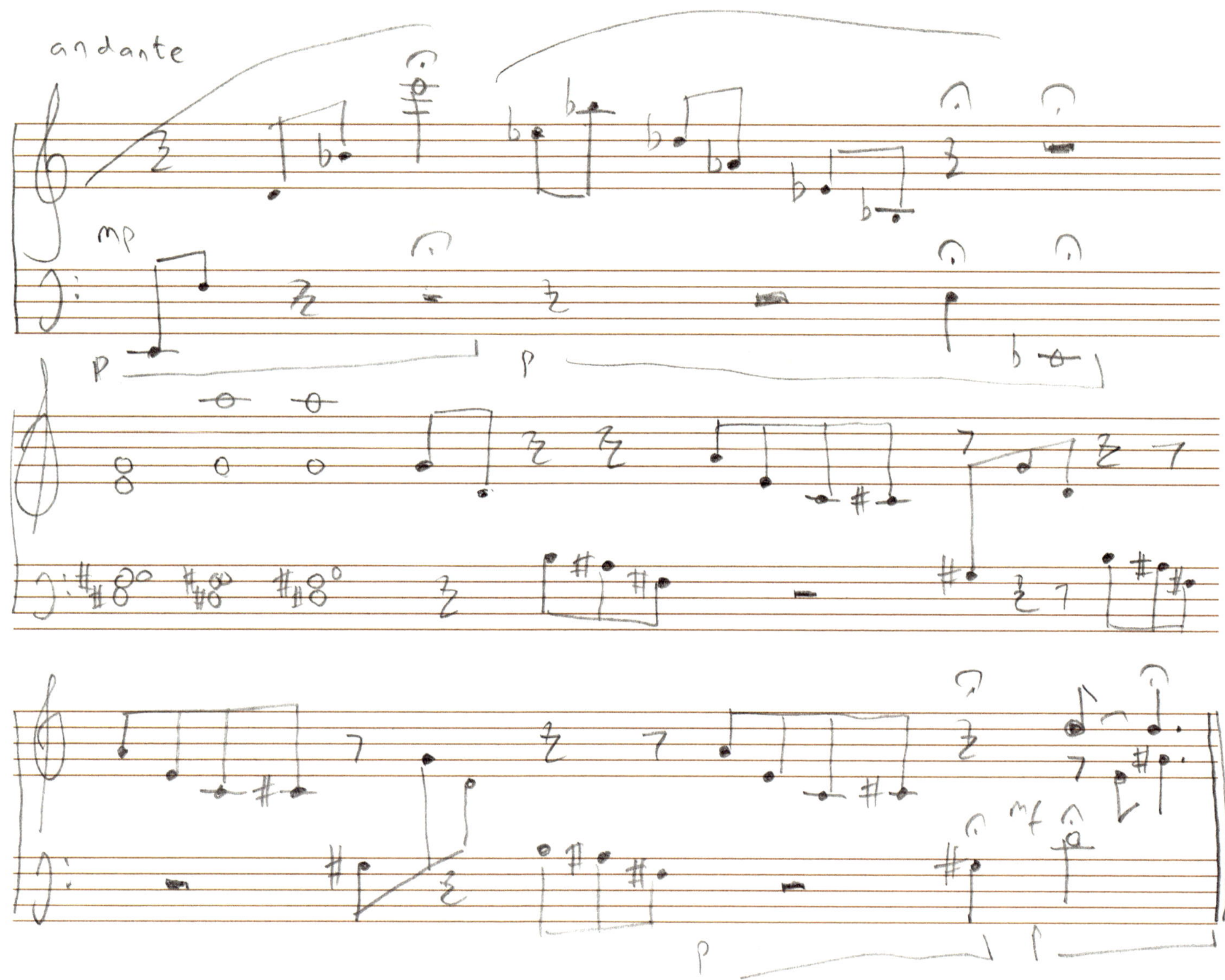
andante
mp
p
p
p
mf

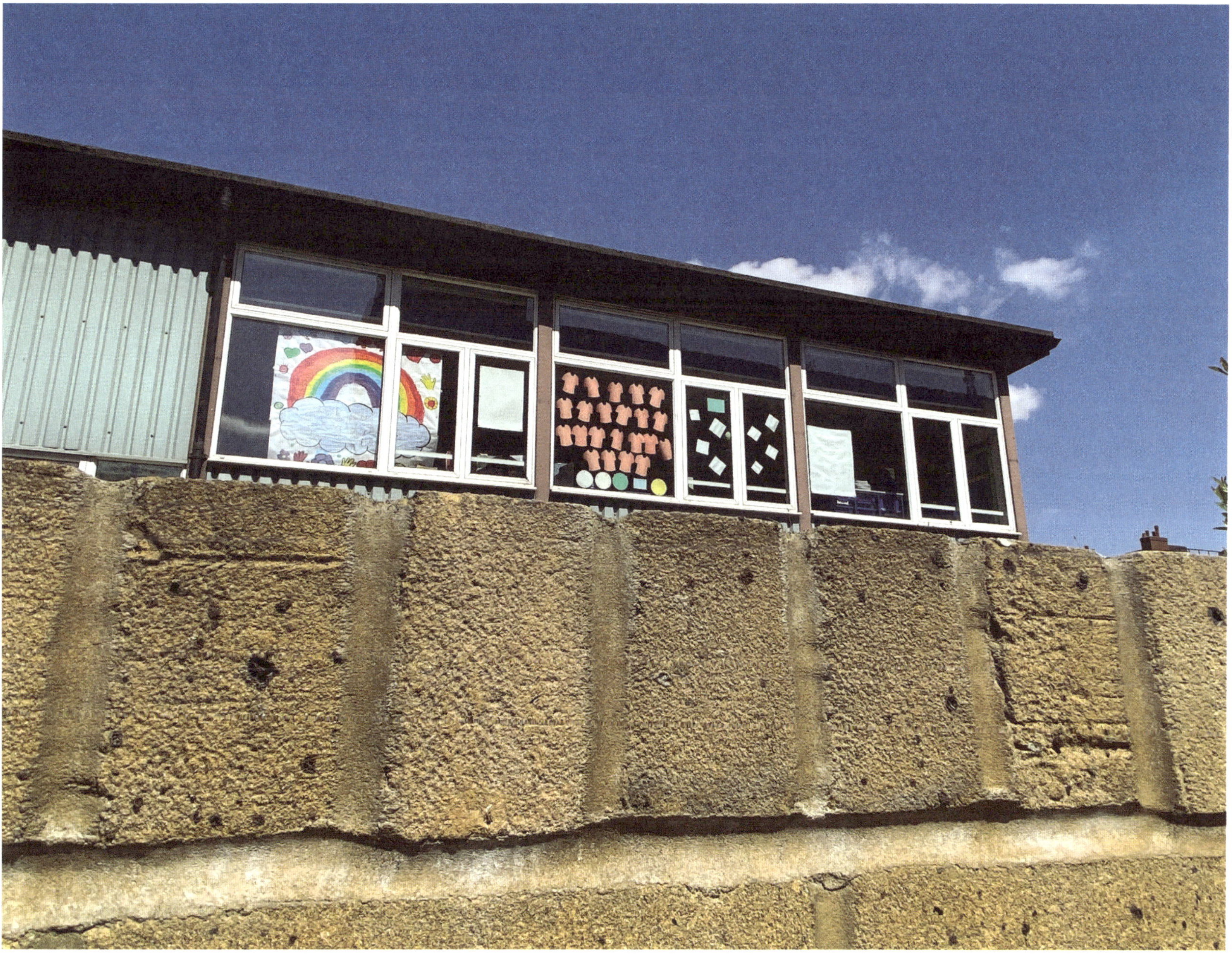

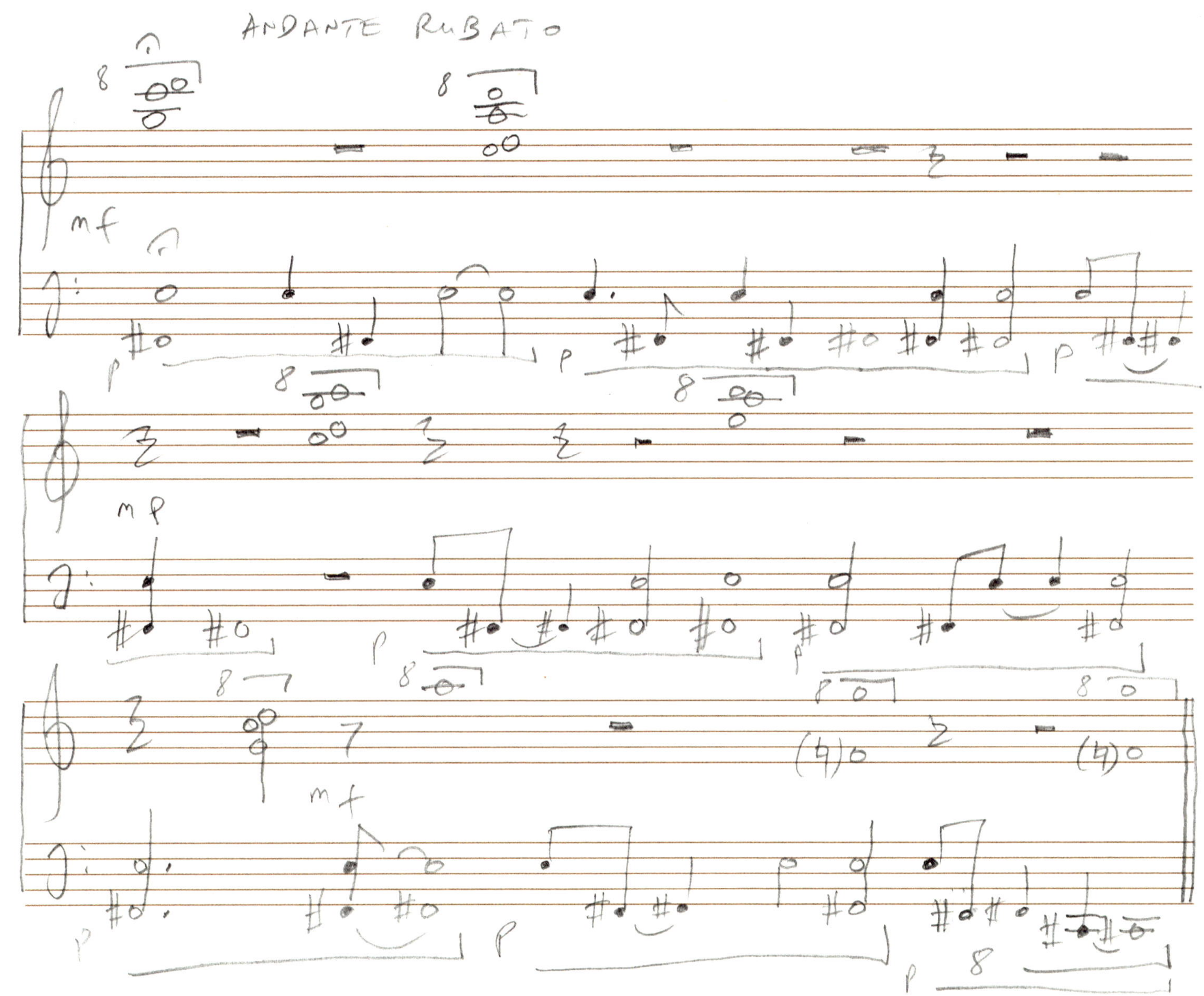
ANDANTE RUBATO
mf
mp
mf

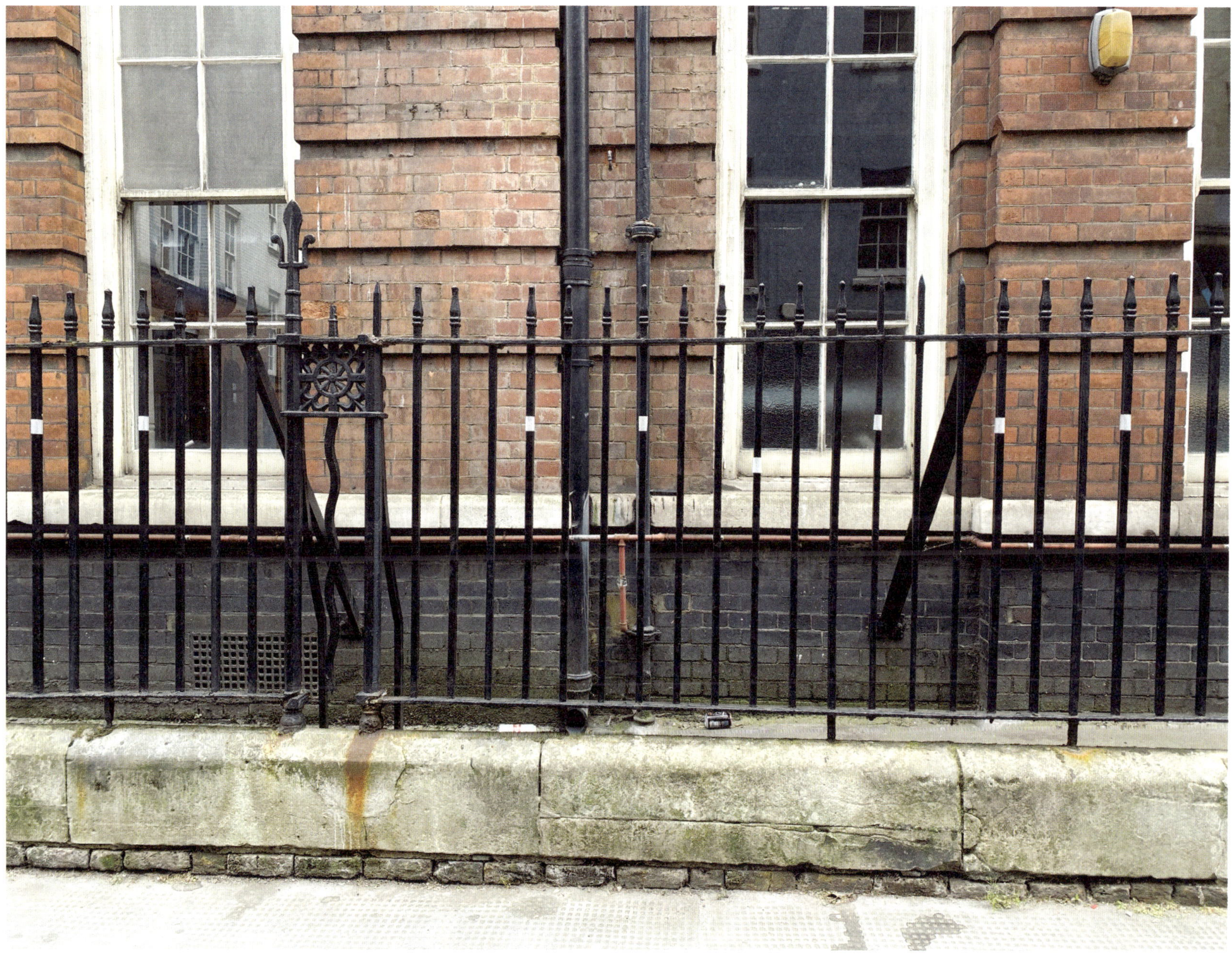

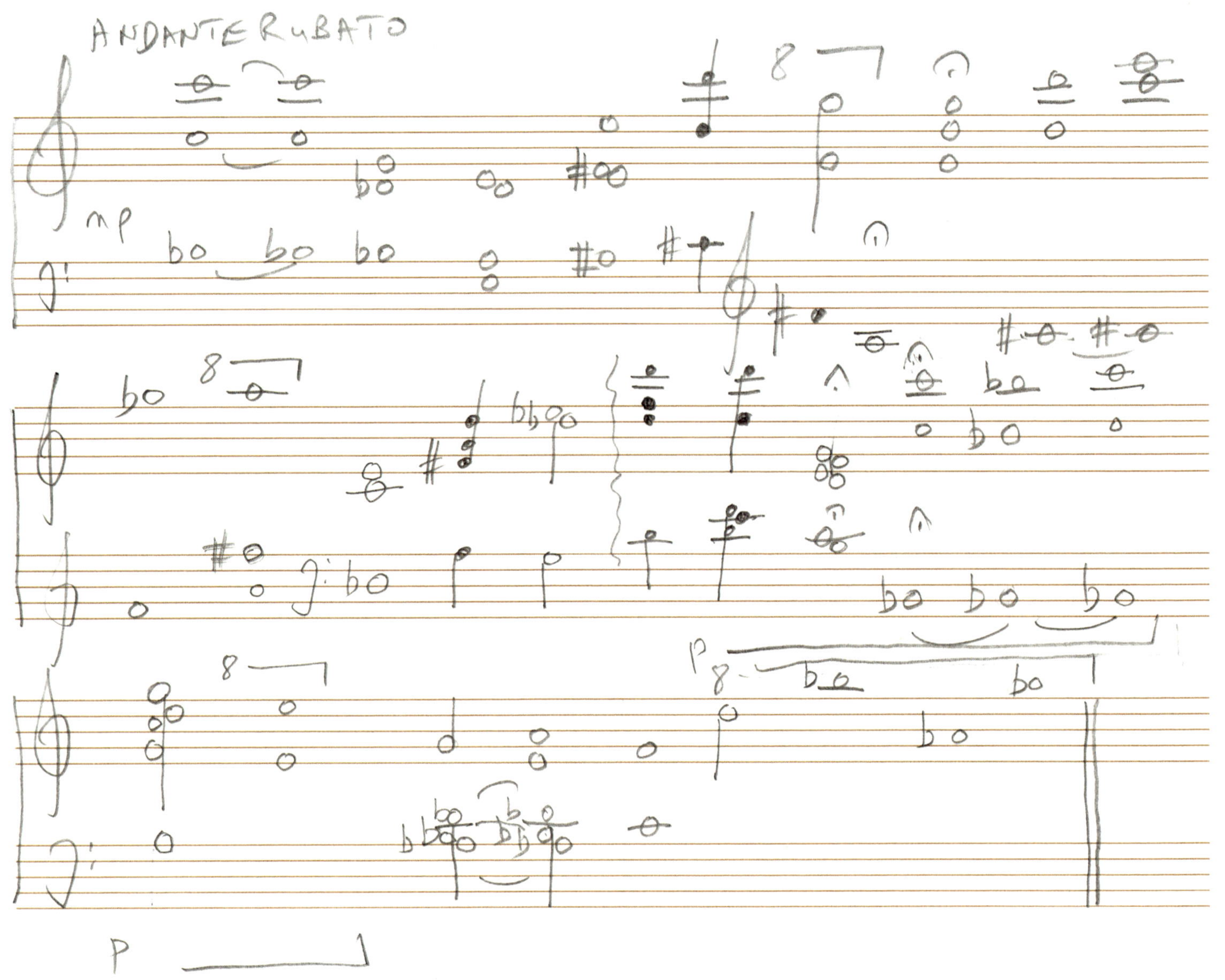
ANDANTE RUBATO
mp
p
p

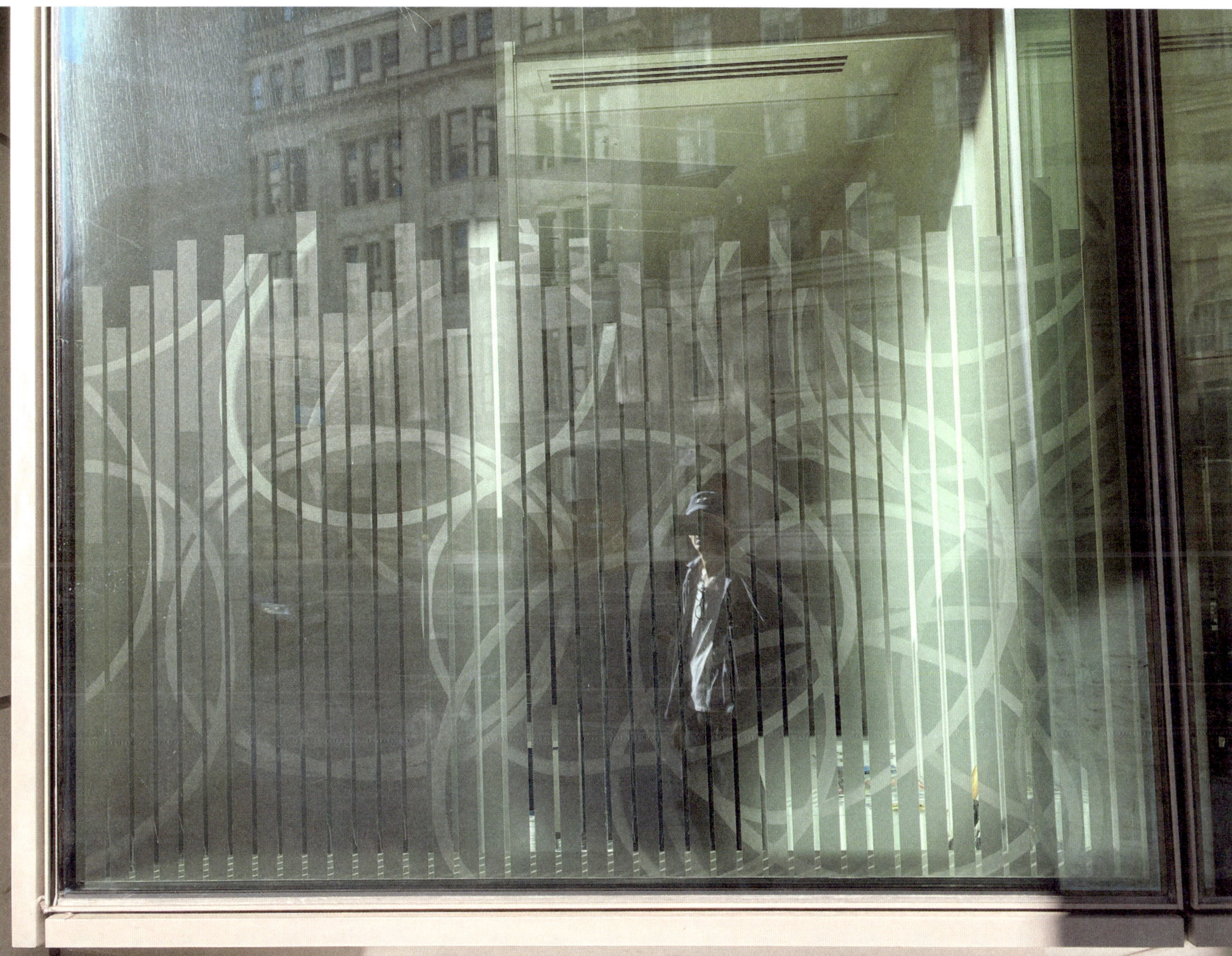

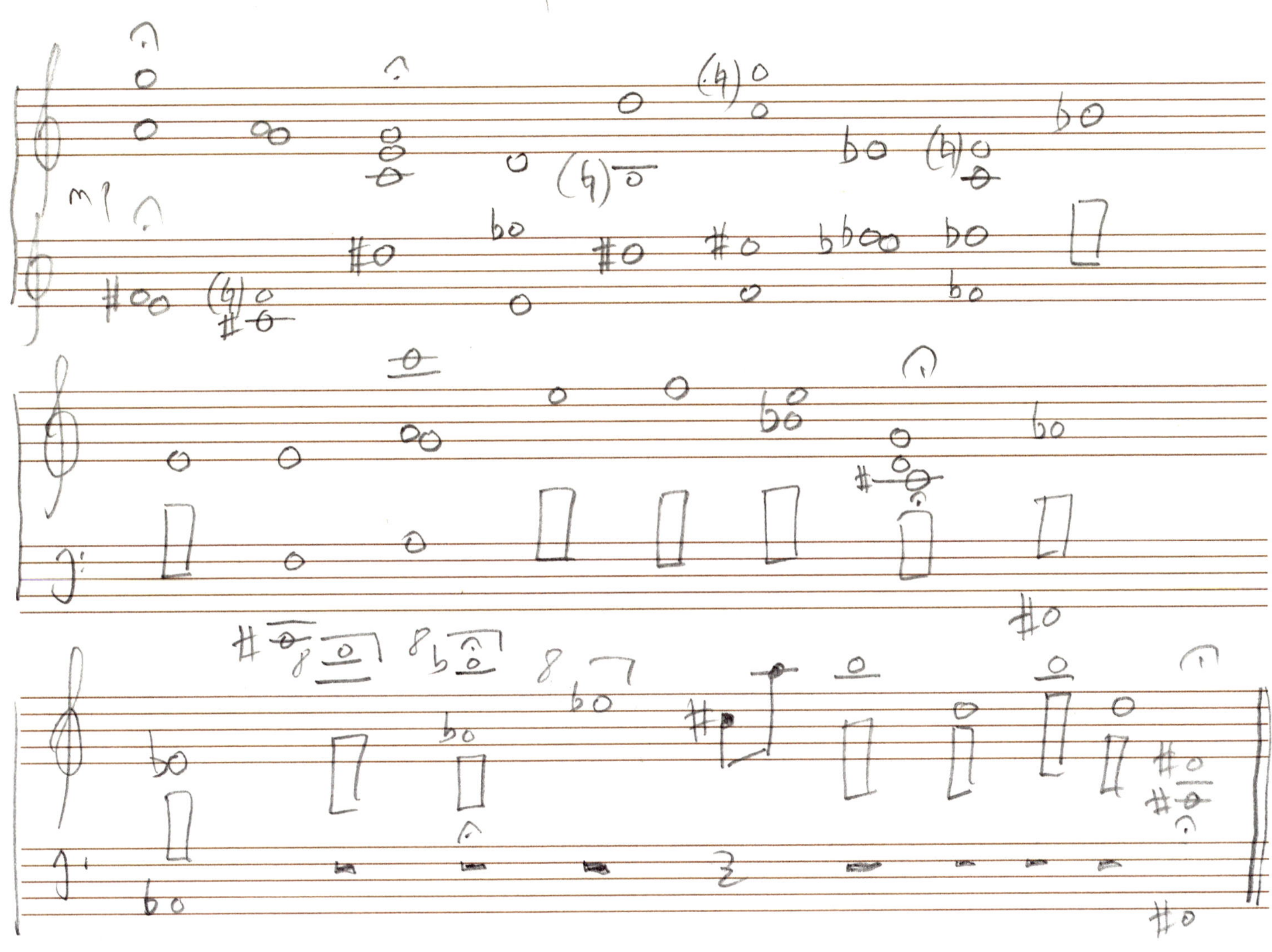
fast rubato
mp

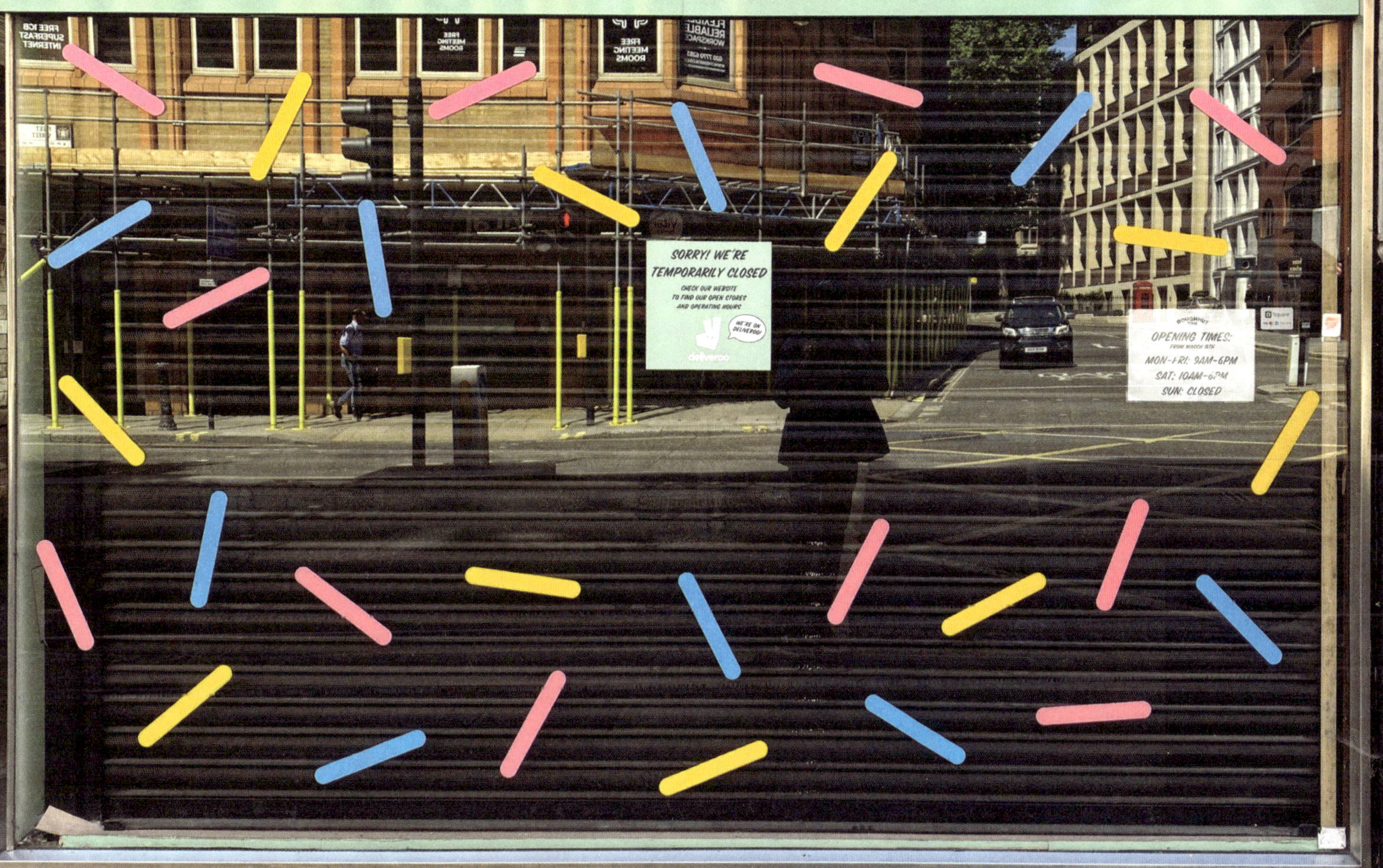
It's always a good time!
SORRY! WE'RE TEMPORARILY CLOSED
CHECK OUR WEBSITE TO FIND OUR OPEN STORES AND OPERATING HOURS
WE'RE ON DELIVEROO!
deliveroo
OPENING TIMES:
MON-FRI: 9AM-6PM
SAT: 10AM-6PM
SUN: CLOSED

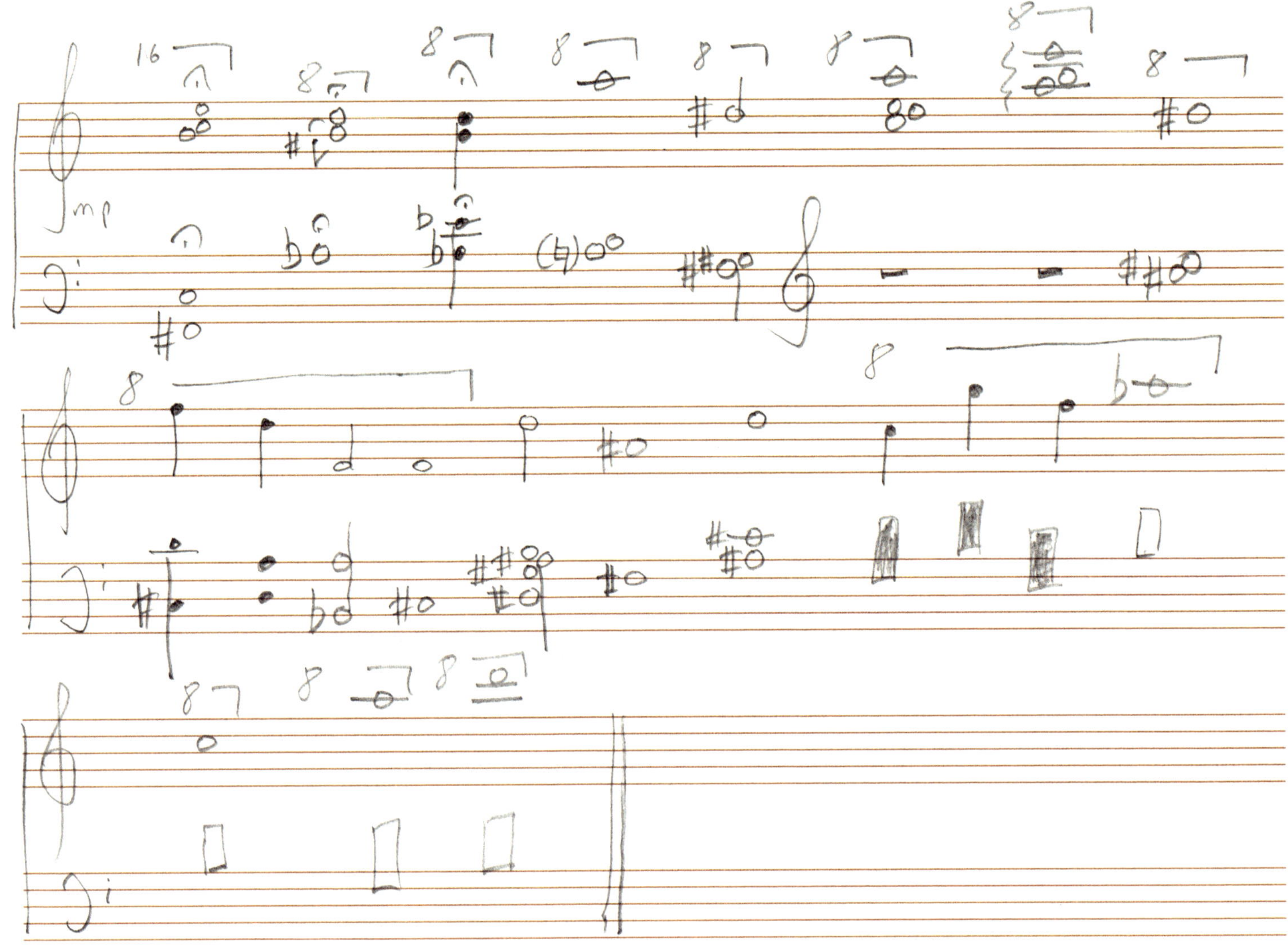
mp

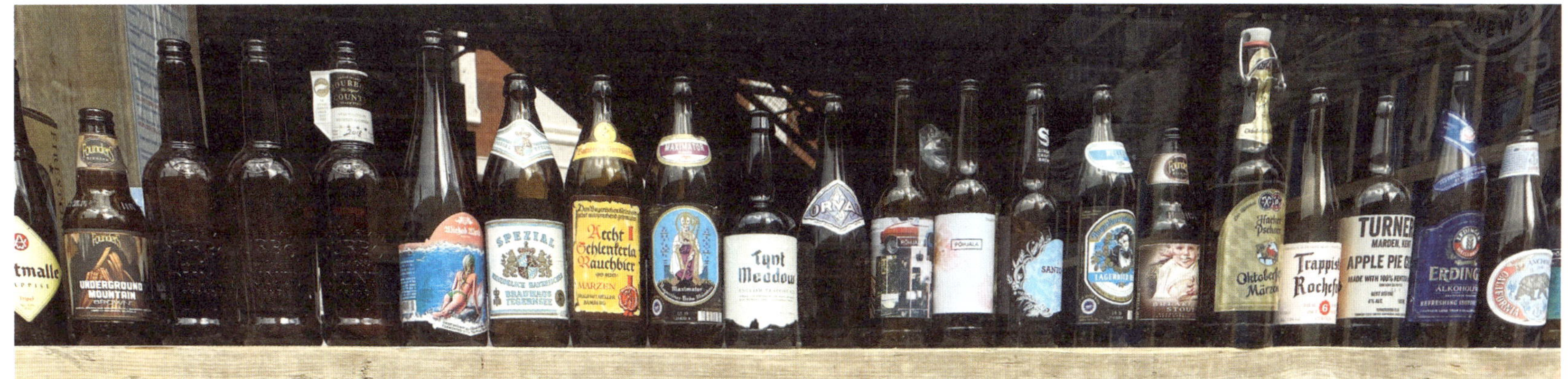
UNDERGROUND MOUNTAIN
SPEZIAL
Aecht Schlenkerla Rauchbier
MÄRZEN
Tynt Meadow
TURNER
APPLE PIE

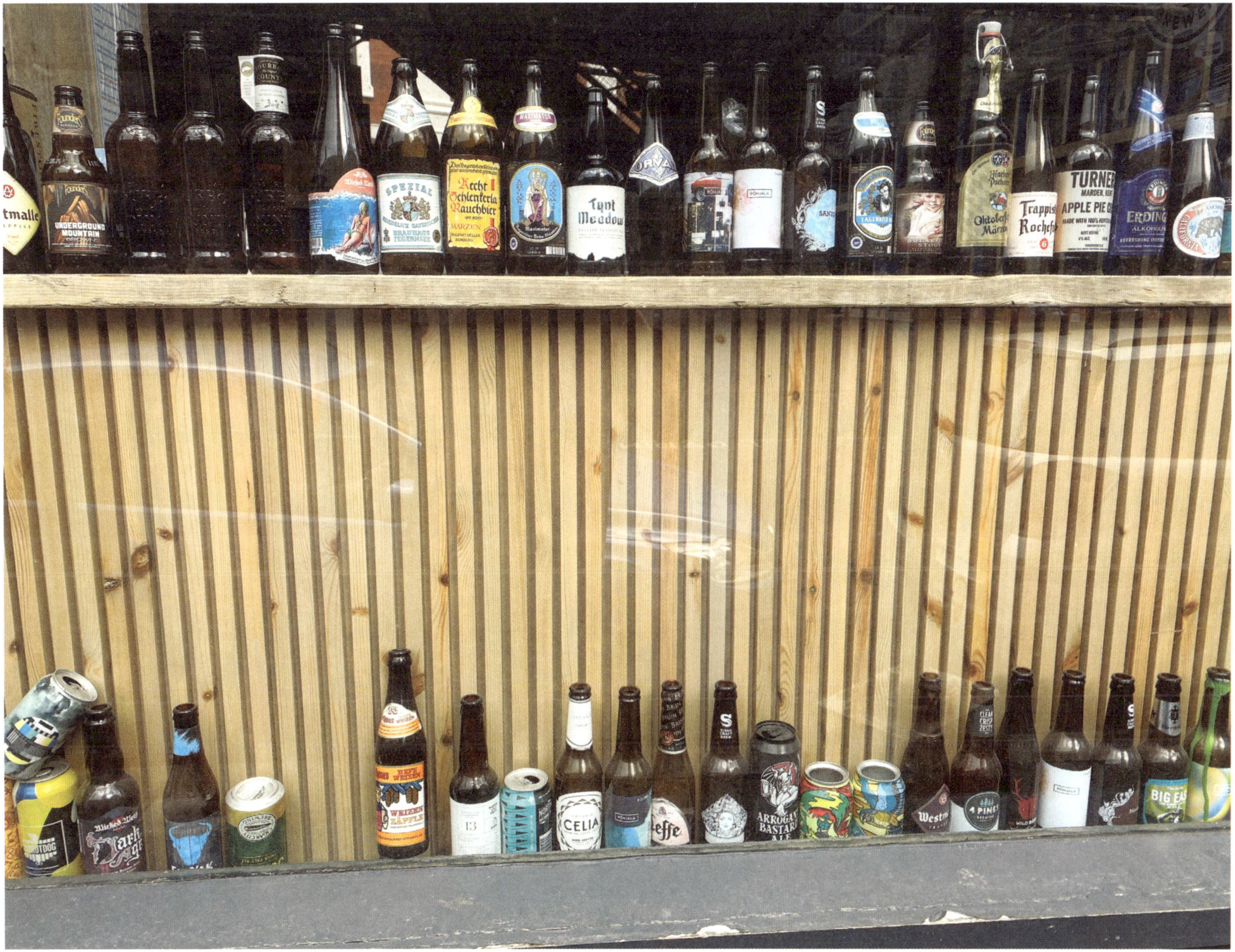

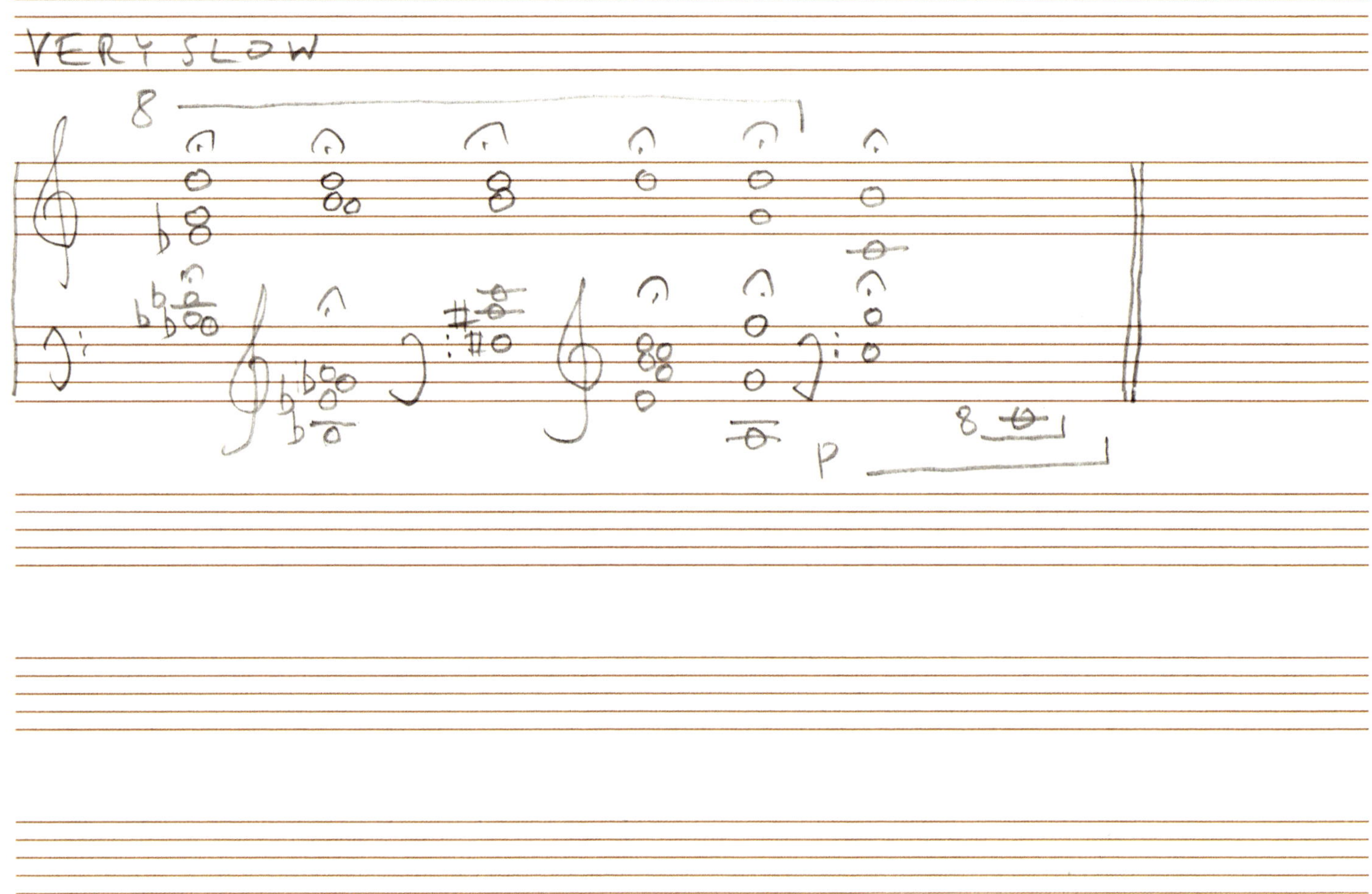
VERY SLOW
p

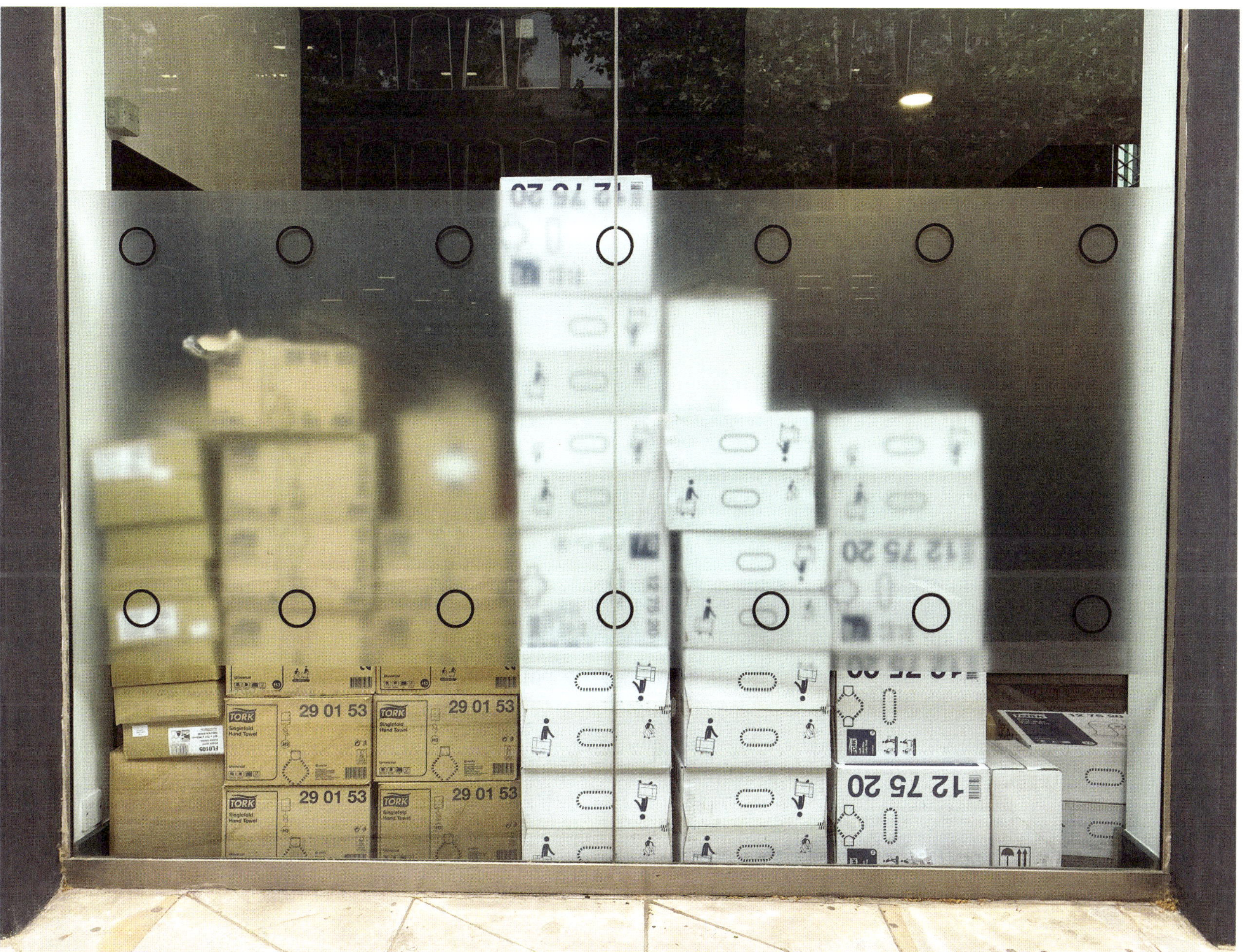

TORK
Singlefold
Hand Towel
29 01 53
TORK
Singlefold
Hand Towel
29 01 53
TORK
Singlefold
Hand Towel
29 01 53
TORK
Singlefold
Hand Towel
29 01 53
12 75 20

Andante rubato

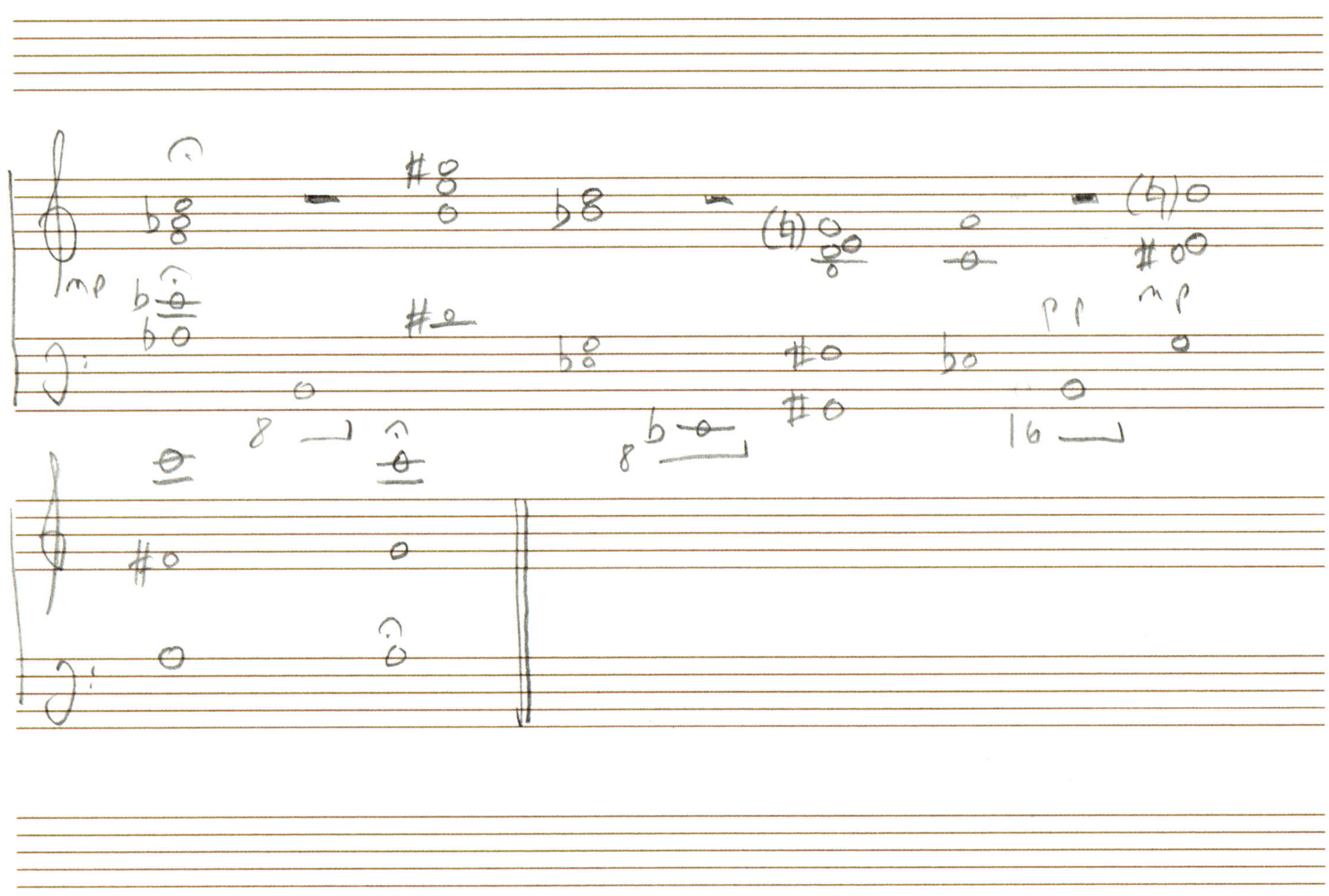

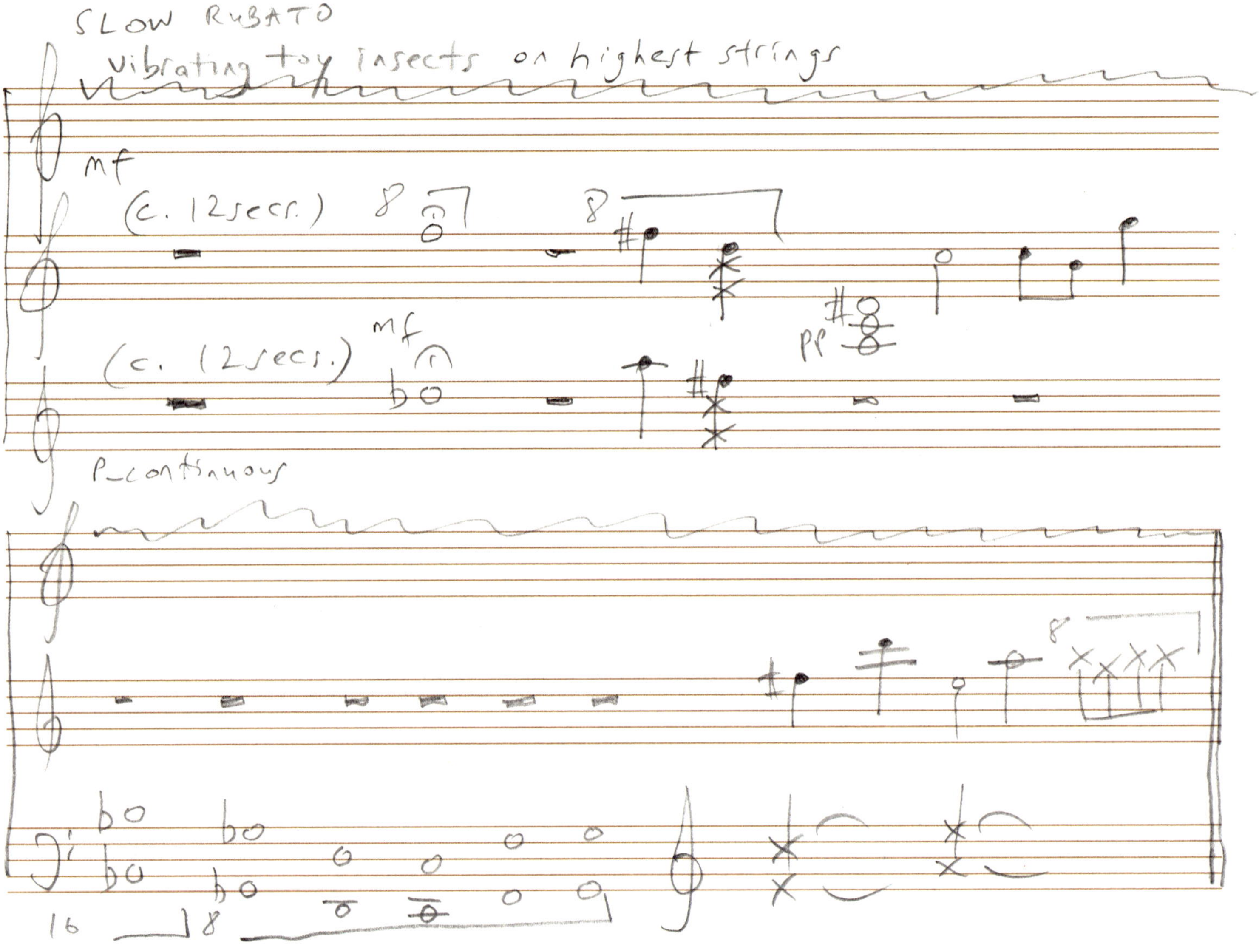

SLOW RUBATO

vibrating toy insects on highest strings

mf

(c. 12secs.) 8 8

pp

(c. 12secs.) mf

p continuous

8

16 8

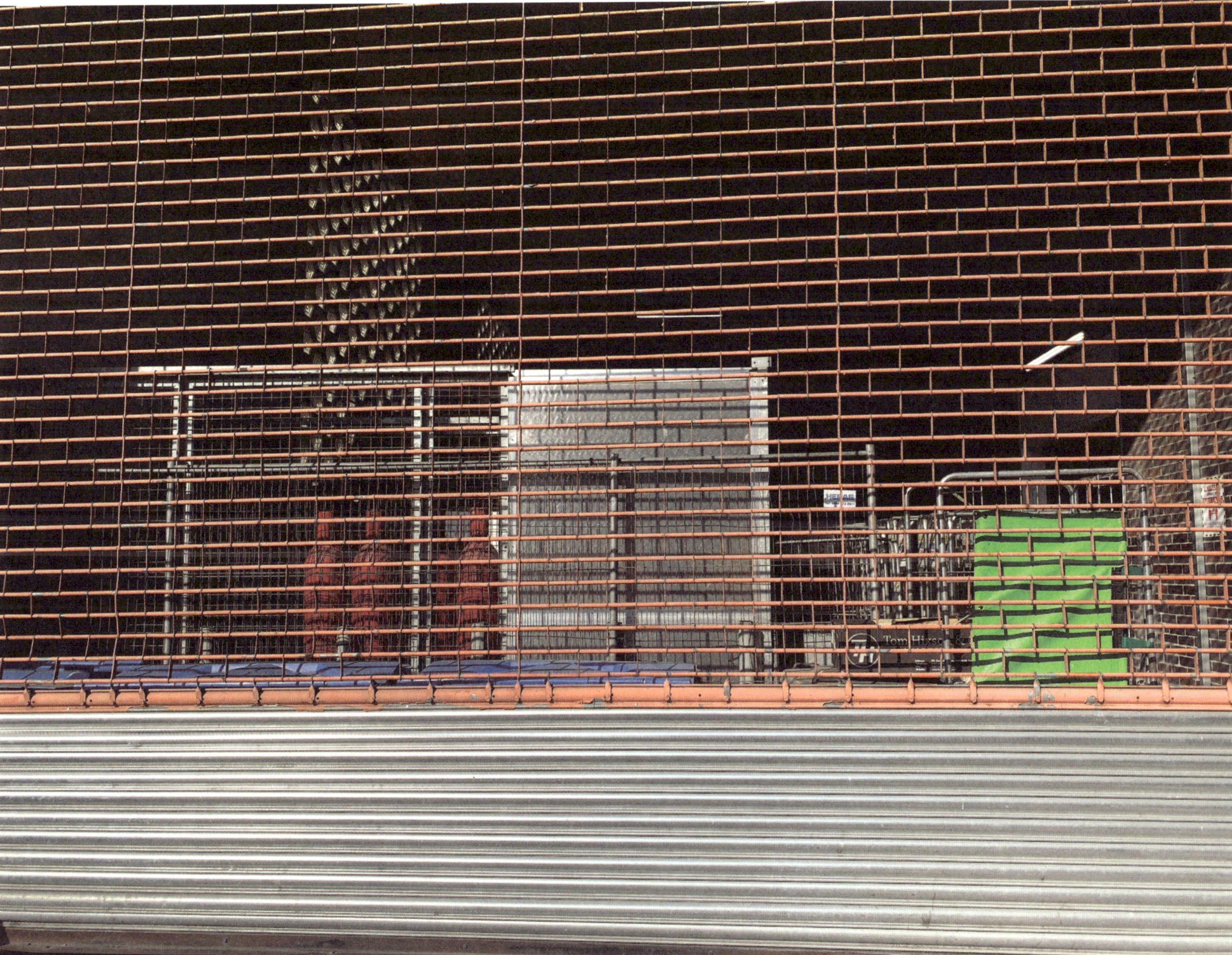

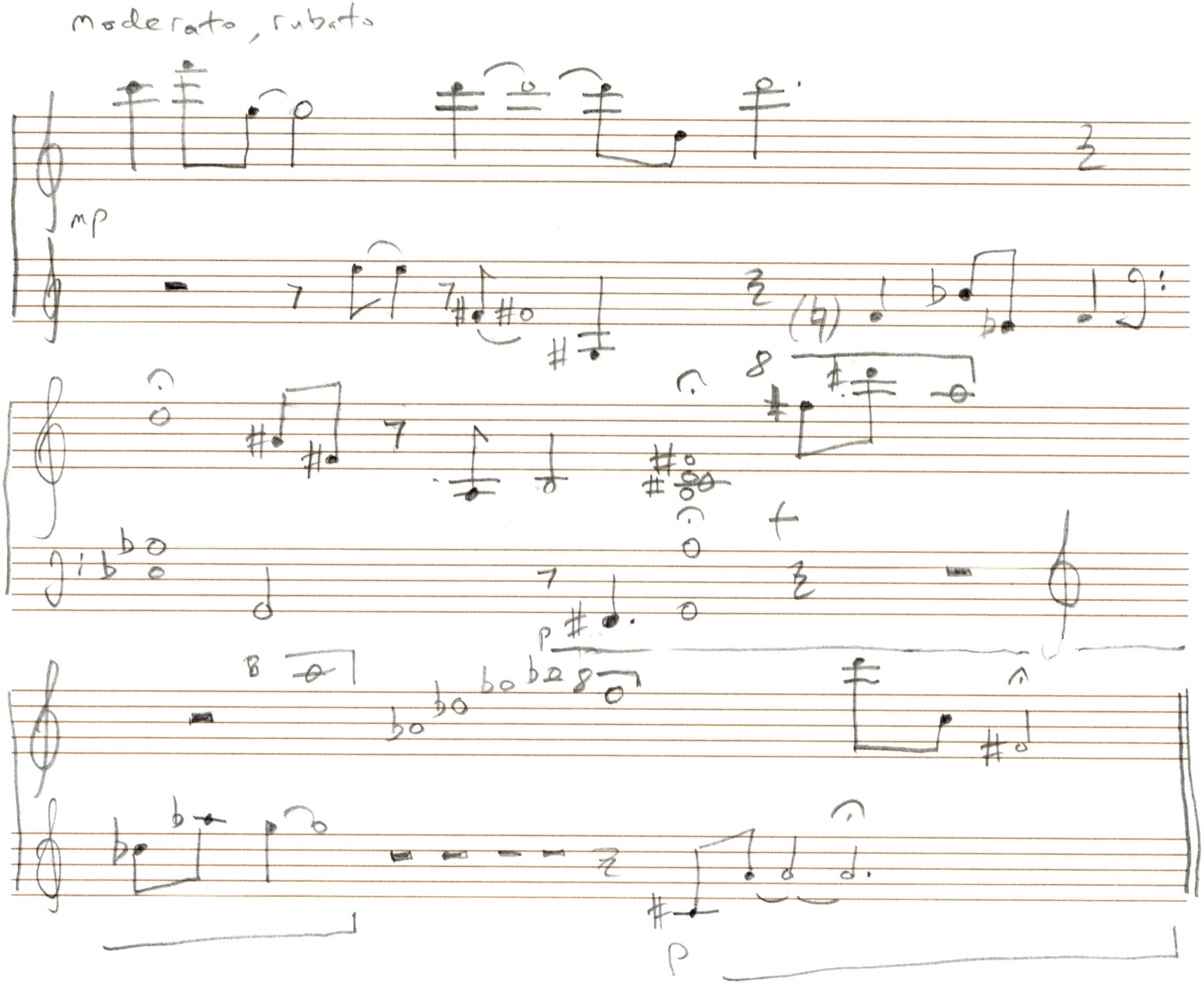

moderato, rubato

mp

8

p

8

p

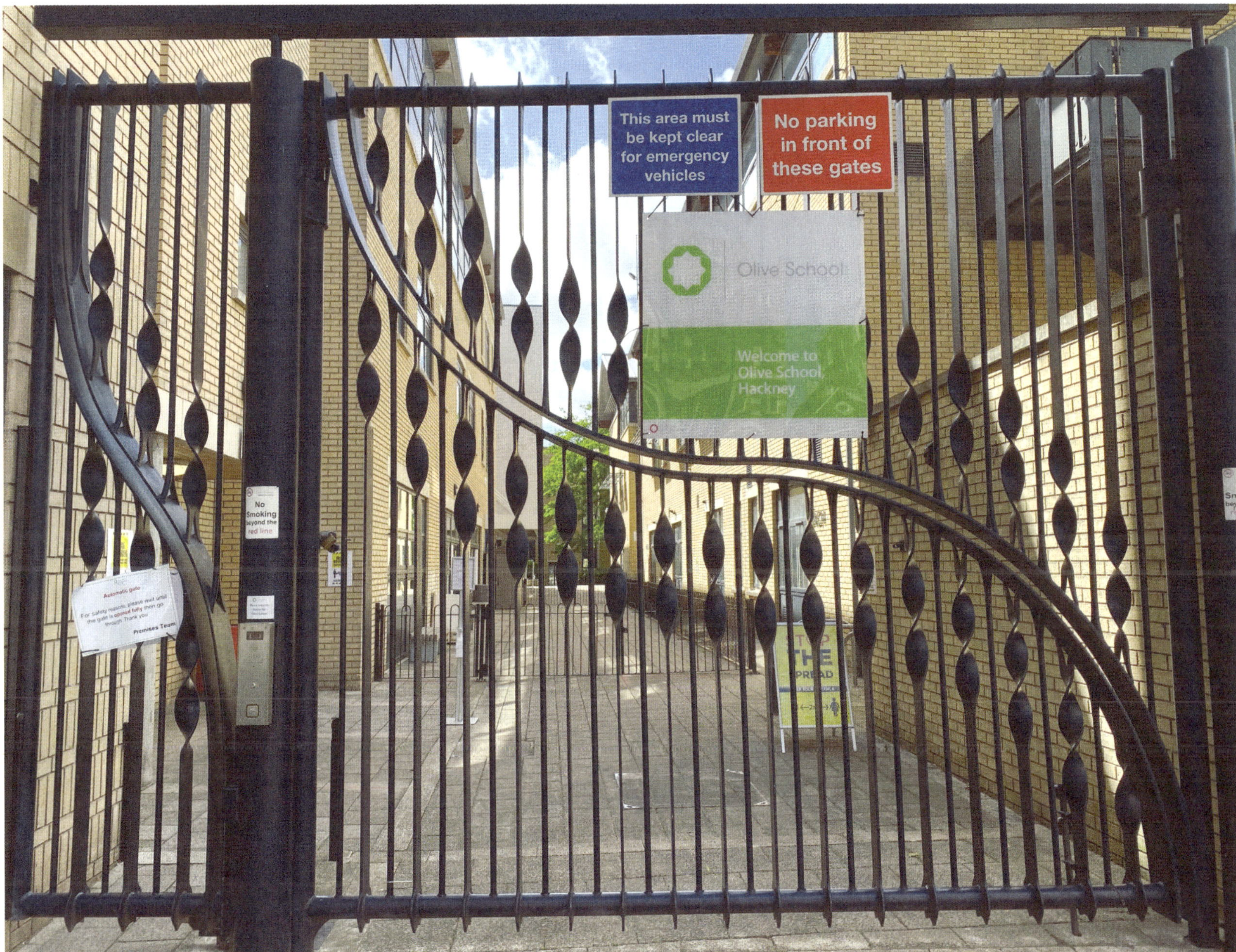
This area must be kept clear for emergency vehicles
No parking in front of these gates
Olive School
Welcome to Olive School, Hackney
No Smoking beyond the red line
Automatic gate
For safety reasons, please wait until the gate is opened fully then go through Thank you
Premises Team

1	Saturday, April 11, 2020	11	Thursday, May 14, 2020
2	Thursday, April 23, 2020	12	Saturday, May 16, 2020
3	Monday, April 27, 2020	13	Sunday, May 17, 2020
4	Tuesday, April 28, 2020	14	Thursday, May 21, 2020
5	Sunday, May 3, 2020	15	Friday, May 22, 2020
6	Monday, May 4, 2020	16	Thursday, May 28, 2020
7	Wednesday, May 6, 2020	17	Monday, June 15, 2020
8	Thursday, May 7, 2020	18	Thursday, June 18, 2020
9	Saturday, May 9, 2020	19	Friday, June 19, 2020
10	Tuesday, May 12, 2020	20	Monday, July 6, 2020

Cover and book design: Christian Marclay and Natalie Kraft

First Edition | ISBN: 978-1-938221-30-9 | Printed and bound in China

siglio uncommon books at the intersection of art & literature
PO BOX 111, Catskill, New York 12414 p: 310-857-6935 www.sigliopress.com

Available to the trade through D.A.P./Artbook.com
75 Broad Street, Suite 630, New York, NY 10004
Tel: 212-627-1999 Fax: 212-627-9484